What People are Saying About "Wealth on the Beach"

Tim Storey, Author, Celebrity Life Coach

"What do you do when you don't know what to do? Daniel Alonzo sets the record straight. This new and dynamic book finally gives us the answers we have all been waiting for. Thank you Daniel for helping us move forward with wisdom and power."

Hector LaMarque, Entrepreneur, Top Sales Trainer

"Daniel Alonzo has written an important book about success and winning. He has created a successful business in Financial Services while helping many create their own success. I've had the pleasure of mentoring Daniel for over 2 decades. He's been a very coachable mentee, as a result, he has written about some of the most important success principles that will help anyone looking to succeed in their life and business. From Mindset to Leadership, Replicating yourself and Mastering Financial Intelligence. You will find valuable nuggets that will guide you in your quest for success in business and creating freedom in your life."

Brandon Dawson, CoFounder, CEO Cardone Ventures

"I've known Daniel for over 20 years and I can testify to his commitment to other peoples personal, professional and financial success."

Chris Howard, National Sales Director

"Daniel and I have been friends for over 20 years, I've watched him go from a kid making seven dollars an hour to becoming a multi-millionaire, top producing sales trainer, business leader

and coach. He's built a great business and developed many successful people because of his solid understanding of people skills, sales skills and leadership skills."

Collis Temple, author, "Work like a Slave, Think like a Master."

"Daniel is real! You get what you see. He's truly a positive person that sees the best in others and believes the best about others. A phenomenal leader that has a tremendous ability to inspire and teach at the same time."

Luis Guico, Regional Vice President, NYSE Company

"Daniel Alonzo has been an integral part of our professional growth in the financial services industry. He has helped thousands of people and continues to do so on a daily basis. He is an inspiration to many, and we are really excited to see him coach more people to become a better version of themselves!"

Angolina Amores, Former Miss Australia

"Kasey is absolutely amazing. I can definitely say that she will relieve any blockages in your life, and pinpoint what you are supposed to do and what your life purpose is. She will answer any questions you have relating to money, relationships, life or anything else. I am truly grateful the universe brought me to her. I was personally feeling stuck, and Kasey helped guide me

to what the universe wanted me to do. Kasey is all about empowering women and will literally transform your life!"

Mahan Shishineh, Former CEO Harcourts Australia

"Wealth on the Beach is insightful, powerful and inspirational. A perfect example of what happens when two great minds collaborate on a subject and produce a well written book.

A must read for anyone!

Ria Prieto, Editor for Inquirer.Net, Lifestyle Influencer and Enthusiast

"Kasey's words are truly inspiring. Her writing is a gift to the world, and has had great influence on all of us."

DJ TonyToni, Broadcaster, Podcaster

"Wealth on the Beach can be for those who are beginning or for those who have years of experience in manifesting. You'll definitely learn more tools to add to your skill set to push you into achieving financial freedom."

Flavio Nuno, Entrepreneur and Investor

"If building a real system for success is the key to winning in business, then it's no wonder that Daniel has succeeded in a huge way."

Vince Ibarra, Entrepreneur and Business Coach

"I've know Daniel for over 15 years. His Leadership and knowledge has helped so many people reach massive success! Daniel leads and that's why he has impacted so many. If you're looking for someone to help your business with reaching its max potential, Daniel Alonzo is for you!"

WEALTH ON THE BEACH™

11 UNIVERSAL LAWS TO BUILDING FINANCIAL FREEDOM

DANIEL ALONZO

WITH KASEY PHOENIX CASAL

Wealth on the Beach

Authorized by The Alonzo Academy. All rights reserved.

©MMXXII

3190-B Shelby Street, Ontario, CA 91764

909-980-8700

Table of Contents

PREFACE 1

ABOUT THE AUTHOR 6

LAW 1 |CREATING THE VISION 11

    Do it NOW!...14

LAW 2 | MINDSET 16

    Making Energy into Money 17

    Creating An Abundance Frequency 19

    Reframing Core Beliefs, To Change Your Current Reality 19

    Changing Your Narrative, Change Your Life.....................20

    Awakening Consciousness: Becoming Aware, Making the Change 21

    Rising Up to the Challenge 22

    Habits & Rituals...23

    Self-Discipline & Organization...........................24

    Mental Toughness, Mental Grit...........................25

    The Struggle is Real 25

LAW 3 | LEADERSHIP...28

    Transforming Your Identity into a Leader...........29

    Moving into Your Greatness 29

    Visualizing and Meeting Your Higher Version of Self.......30

    Self Awareness | Being Authentic in Your Mission, Finding Purpose, Creating Lasting Change..31

Understanding the Laws of Energy, Karma and Intentions | Giving to Receive..33

Learning the Rules to Redefine the Rules..........................35

Boss or a Leader? Know the Difference 36

Moving from an Employee Mentality to Leader | Leading from The Front 37

Shed the Ego, Win the War 37

Release the Need for Control...39

Remembering Why You Started | Believe in Your Contribution and Impact to The World 40

Let's talk about Accountability...43

LAW 4 | QUALITIES OF THE WEALTHY 45

Setting Your Frequency, Maintaining New Character 45

Doing What Others Are Not Willing to Do, No Excuses...46

Time is A Luxury | Using Your Time Wisely 48

Discipline | Doing What You Say You Will Do 49

Consistency & Patience | It's All About Being Excitedly Patient..50

Grit | Mental Toughness and Resilience.............................51

Are you Mentally tough? 52

Lead With Integrity, Aligning Your Values with Purpose ..54

Value Experience Over Things...56

Remembering Where You Came From | Stay Humble, But Hungry 57

Focus On Continuous Self Improvement..........................58

Automate Your Life..59

Health = Wealth...60

STRESS 61

LAW 5 |MASTERING YOUR CRAFT.......................................63

Immerse Yourself in Your Passions...............................63

Mastering Knowledge, Skills & the Discipline 65

Defining Your Niche 66

Finding a Mentor, Replicating Their Moves.......................69

Engaging a Coach 71

Finding and Investing in a Coach 71

LAW 6 | YOUR NETWORK IS YOUR NET WORTH............74

Create a Strong Inner Circle....................................75

Master Talking to Strangers & Aligning with the Right
Vibration..77

Building New Relationships 78

Aligning Your Values, Finding Your People 78

Strengthening Connections 79

Expanding Your Network...81

Maintaining Social Grace in All Your Interactions 81

Becoming Emotionally Intelligent 82

Sharing Your Wealth 83

Say Thank You 83

Say I'm Sorry 84

LAW 7 | LIFTING PEOPLE UP.....................................85

Why Get Positive? 89

3 Stress-Relieving Tips from Norman Vincent Peale 90

One Recruit Away from an Explosion 92

Six Foot Trophies 94

Connection & Love 94

Boss vs. Leader 95

LAW 8 | MASTERING THE SALES GAME............................97

Becoming A Prospecting Master...................................97

Prospect as a Way of Life.......................................98

The World of Social Media 99

But I'm not Computer Savvy....................................101

Are You Afraid of Sales?.......................................102

Understanding Your Market....................................102

Calendly.com...103

The BEST Referral System....................................104

Setting Appointments...105

Are you TYING people down? 107

The Closing Process..109

LAW 9 |REPLICATING THE PROCESS 110

Create the Vision 111

Sell The Dream..112

Maslow's Hierarchy of Needs 112

Replicate Results by Training and Testing Your Team.....113

TRAIN, TRAIN, TRAIN 114

How to Replicate the Process..............................115

1999 116

Tell Your People How YOU Did It 117

A Whole NEW World.......................................118

Different Types of Scaling and Replicating the Process ..119

The McDonald Brothers.....................................121

LAW OF NATURE - PARETO PRINCIPLE 122

LAW 10 | MASTERING FINANCIAL INTELLIGENCE.....124

Good Debt Vs. Bad Debt 125

The RULE of 72..126

High Cost of Waiting 127

Thou Shall Budget 129

Never Use Cash..130

Creating Financially Successful Habits 131

Burn that Money 132

Deduct it Deduct it Deduct it! 138

A Note About Life Insurance 139

The Theory of Decreasing Responsibility.............141

LAW 11 | CREATING LASTING WEALTH 143

Someone Will Need YOU One Day......................144

Well Frequency and Vibration for Life 145

Desperation 146

Alignment..146

Multiply Your Way to Freedom 147

Stock Market 148

Property & Rentals..149

Building an Investment Portfolio 150

Cryptocurrency..152

THE GOAL OF GENERATIONAL WEALTH...............154

Why Build Lasting Wealth? 155

ACKNOWLEDGEMENTS.......................................161

LEGAL DISCLAIMER..162

THANK YOU FOR BUYING THIS BOOK! 164

PREFACE

When The Dream Becomes the Corporate Nightmare

So, you've done the right thing. You've created your cookie-cutter picture-perfect life. You finished your degree, graduated with a 4.0 GPA, landed a gig working your 'dream' job for a corporate giant firm. You went on to marry your 'dream' partner and managed to have two kids, a white picket fence house in the upper-middle-class suburban area you always drove by in your early days in your beat-up Toyota. But now you've upgraded to your Audi and family Range Rover Sport.

Finally, you made it! You're living the 'dream.'

But then slowly, the bills start coming in, your lifestyle expenses start piling up, and anxiety starts kicking in. You realize you're locked into a mortgage for 30 years paying interest to the bank for three-quarters of that time. Recognizing more than half of your income is going towards tax and interest with little to save for your family. You start arguing over petty things with your partner and hate coming home, so you stay at the office working 10–12-hour days in your corner office to escape the environment at home, the pile of dishes, and dirty laundry that you haven't been able to clean. All this because you're trying to climb the corporate ladder, become the youngest executive in the business, get a measly $10,000 pay rise, and please a boss you hate.

Not really the grand dream that it panned out to be now, is it? This was the life of Kasey Phoenix Casal. A young and ambitious young mom who managed to get into the best University in Australia, completing a double degree in HR & Psychology, finishing her Masters, and working for the biggest Corporate Banks and HR Recruitment Firms in Australia.

Despite the hurdles she faced in her teen years, she did everything right. She had been expelled from three private schools by fourteen, pregnant at sixteen, engaged at eighteen, and living in the poorest suburbs of Australia, where everyone lived on welfare. She strived to make something of herself, have a better life and sought to build 'the great dream.' Because that is the image we are sold. So, she got into the university and worked her ass off for five years while taking care of a young family and working in the biggest bank in Australia. She thought she had made it. But every single day, she would drive to work with the eerie feeling that something wasn't right. The bills would pile up every month. She would drown her sorrows with alcohol and get stressed from the upcoming reports, meetings, and projects she had to deliver in the coming weeks.

Eventually, the great dream became a nightmare.

While she looked picture perfect on the outside, there was some aspect of Kasey desperately seeking a way out. Every day she would drive to work in her ideal car, in her perfect outfit and heels, to her 'perfect' job… with no other thought in her mind other than to drive her car straight into a brick wall.

Now tell me, is this the great dream after all? Is this what you want to be striving for from the minute you get out of school or college?

She had been appointed as the youngest HR executive in her company at twenty-six, sitting in the boardroom with the big guys and given the 'corner' office with city skyline views. But it didn't take long before she would shut her office door every day, look out the window, and cry - hoping for a way out. Her family was falling apart with a second baby on the way. She was managing a stressful project at work to restructure and terminate management lines and put people on performance management. Not to mention she was way over her head in consumer credit card debt (blame Chanel and LV). After this, who cares about climbing the corporate ladder and breaking glass ceilings. What a shit fucking job. And what a bullshit life this turned out to be. This dream had quickly turned into a world-class nightmare. Tell me, can you relate?

This is, unfortunately, the lifestyle that the majority of white-collar professionals work towards. To create a cookie-cutter life working 9-5 that quickly becomes strife. Most working professionals never see the end of the rat race, working every single day of their lives tirelessly to make the taxman and the banks rich. Only to be burned out, stressed, and low-key depressed. So why do so many people still strive to live this 'great American dream?' You have to ask yourself, is this genuinely living life?

We've all been fed a bunch of lies about what it means to be a success. We've all been fed lies about what it means to be wealthy and free and that it's unachievable. If you think about the average person, you will see someone who finishes college with debt, only to get into more debt when they purchase a house and be confined to a lifelong mortgage. That house you just bought isn't even yours until you've paid for it in full! The bank owns the title, so the bank and your job own you, thirty years to life!

Something has to change. The mindset, beliefs, and ways of living and thinking of our generation and the ones before us have been programmed that being part of this system is normal. This is the way of life. But what if there was another way of living? One where you can live truly free, travel whenever and wherever you want, spend more time with your loved ones, and have income coming regardless of whether you're 'pounding the pavement' and working? What if you can acquire massive amounts of income streams and build a genuine nest egg and generational wealth for you and your family and children? What if you could actually LIVE LIFE before your retirement and actually experience things without worrying about paying back debt, or your next monthly salary payment, and whether you'll make a bonus or not? Ask yourself, what if.

Wealth on the Beach is your key to FREEDOM. It's your key to happiness. It's your key to life.

They say money is the root of all evil. But that is a blatant lie. In fact, money is what value you add to it. Money only highlights a person's character and intentions and can allow a person to come into their true self. If you build wealth and have passive income, you can create the lifestyle of your dreams, be able to take care of your family, friends, and loved ones, and not have to live in a scarcity mindset or survival. And actually, be whoever the fuck you want to be.

So why wouldn't you take the leap? Why would you settle for working a 9-5 job for $100,000 a year and live on a budget every single day of your limited time here for 40+ years, only to die with a substandard life, shallow experiences, and no wealth to pass on to your children? That, to me, is crazy, and that is why this book has been created. To provide you with a step-by-step blueprint for gaining true wealth, passive income, and freedom!

I am Daniel Alonzo, I've helped thousands of people escape the rat race, and now I want to help you. This is my gift to enlighten you and awaken you to truly live your life on your terms. To give you my blueprint and my personal journey to help you get out of your corporate nightmare - and into financial freedom.

About the Author

Daniel Alonzo

Entrepreneur, businessman, investor, public speaker, trainer, and coach. Daniel started from humble beginnings and came from a modest working-class family. He wasn't a trust fund kid or born with a silver spoon. His early days started with an ambition to become an athlete, but a fated knee injury caused him to retire from this dream and ended his promising journey in baseball. The irony is that if it had not been for this tragic event and coming home defeated and depressed, he would not have found the path to entrepreneurship and wealth - or be who he is today.

Coming back home, feeling useless and unmotivated after his injury, he felt miserable and like a total loser. It wasn't until his childhood best friend called him up with a business opportunity with a financial company that he began feeling like he had purpose again. He went to an event to hear about the business proposition with nothing to lose. In the beginning, he thought it sounded like a scam and cringe-worthy infomercial about getting financially independent, having financial freedom, and making tons of money.

Daniel thought, '*what a bunch of bullshit.*'

But some part of his conscience was pushing him, something in his gut, maybe the Universe, and he said, 'what's the worst that could happen, you got nothing to lose and everything to gain.'

So, he went for it!

So, at the tender age of twenty-one, he was already set on the path to creating a different life and following a road less traveled. I mean, it's not like he was doing anything else remotely exciting with his life post-injury.

A year went by, and nothing much had taken off or happened. At that age, he was half committed and didn't really know anything about business or have any strong mentors around him. So, the motivation was low.

But finally, one day, he woke up and committed to going all in. He reached out to one of the most successful people in the business and, straight up, asked him for coaching. Daniel was an athlete, so he was very coachable and mentally tough. So, the mentor agreed to coach him. It was then that Daniel was given the blueprint to freedom. Step-by-step the whole process - beginning to end.

Seeing the potential of this scalable business model in gaining residual, passive income, he worked his fucking ass off. Although, in the beginning, Daniel was out there all hours of the night, getting rejection after rejection. He still pushed himself, thinking, no one would be willing to go through all this rejection, and most people would have surely given up by now. But Daniel didn't. And that's when he knew he would make it. He was willing to do everything that most people wouldn't. Pursuing temporary discomfort for permanent freedom.

"You may not be where you want to be, but thank God you are not where you used to be."

Tim Storey

After a couple of years of putting in the focused, determined, passion-filled effort, he started to make $100K a year! He was only twenty-four years old.

The following year he made $170K. The next year, $250k. The next year, $350K, and by age twenty-eight, Daniel made $500K in a single year. (That's almost $800K in today's dollars) The significant part was that he made that primarily passive. And due to him practicing what he was preaching, inflation adjusted, he amassed a $1.5 million dollar nest-egg! Since then, his income has kept skyrocketing. Today, Daniel has amassed true wealth and actual residual, passive income by diversifying in different income streams via rental income, mutual funds, trading stocks, options, venture capital, and cryptocurrency. But 50% of Daniel's recurrent and residual income still comes from his core business, financial services.

Today, Daniel teaches and trains aspiring entrepreneurs and people who want to get out of the 9-5 rat race to scale their businesses faster, build similar wealth, and have fun! Daniel oversees fifty locations, and his team recruits 3,000 plus people per year.

Daniel's success came because of two things. He mastered his craft, pushed others, and never gave up. In the industry, he's one of the best at what he does and has done speaking events across North America on building an income that never stops. His business expertise is how to replicate any business model. Taking over small companies and transforming them into a much bigger business with recurring passive income. From all this, Daniel has also mastered managing his money, resources, and reinvesting to grow his net worth.

His business services approximately 500 families a month through insurance and investments. The business has over $350 million in assets under management, issued billions in life insurance face amount & paid out $151 million in claims to families. Daniel has built a net worth of over $20 Million to date.

The defining moment for Daniel was while he was in college, still green in the business. He was taking a math class, and his final exam took place during a convention for his company the same day. He asked his professor if he could take the exam another day.

The professor replied, "If you don't show up, you will fail the class."

At that moment, he made the life-altering decision to quit college and go all-in on his dream of financial freedom. It was a risk, but he never looked back. That turned out to be the best decision he ever made. Never wanting to be defined by a piece of paper from college or have anyone dictate what he can or can't do in life. He was stepping into true, liberating freedom. And that freedom came from wanting to not be just another cog in 'the system.'

Daniel didn't finish college. He didn't get a degree. But he did become one of the top 1% earners in North America. This is the story of Daniel and his journey to financial freedom. And this book is his step-by-step manual on how you can ultimately do it too.

LAW 1 |CREATING THE VISION

"There's no shortage of money, only of people thinking big enough."

Grant Cardone

L et me start off by asking you. What would you be doing today if money were no object? Would you be working on the job you are working at today? Or would you be doing something else? Serious question. Stop for a minute and consciously think about the life you have created for yourself so far. Is it everything that you had hoped it would be? Are you living the lifestyle that you have dreamed of? Do you have the freedom of time and choice? Be honest. If you can't give a straight answer, then we know your answer. Simple. The sad reality of society, even as evolved as we are today, is that we are all still limited in our ability to truly create the life of our dreams. You believe that we are free in the choices that we make. But are you really?

The great 'American Dream' that has been sold to us from day one is like the story of what most people are taught. Get a decent degree, get a job, get married, get a white picket fence house in the suburbs, have two or three kids, two cars, and settle. So, you find a decent corporate job, get a six-figure salary, build a half-decent version of yourself, and call this 'success' in life. But is this truly what you are passionate about? Do you jump out of bed at the thought of this so-called successful life? If the answer is yes, then there is absolutely no need for you to keep reading these chapters, and by all means, I'm truly happy for you! If this is what you have strived for, and you can say at the end of your days that you are happy with the life you've created, the multi-million-dollar nest egg you've built, and the person you've become, then congratulations! You have made it.

But for those of you seeking and striving for something more, this book is the answer for you. You see, we've all been hardwired to live a lie. It is a vision that has been imprinted on us from birth of what it truly means to be successful. True success comes from living life to the fullest and living life on your own terms. True success comes from financial freedom. Now for the majority of you, you will say - money isn't everything, and it doesn't equal happiness. You are absolutely right. Money doesn't equal happiness, money equals options. It is the vehicle to provide you with the freedom to live life the way you have always dreamed of and become the person you were meant to become. To get out of your corporate nightmare. To get out of that 9-5 job that you hate!

Be whoever the fuck you want to be. Life shouldn't be limited to what your bosses think about you or your colleagues, friends, family. What if you decide to wake up and be your authentic self one day? Choose to build your income based on your passion and purpose, creating recurring income. Instead of working in that 9-5 you hate and barely make enough to get by. What if you were able to create the life of your dreams, make an impact and create a legacy, instead of conforming to what society expects you to be?

Too often, we have boxed ourselves in because of the opinion of others around us - unsupportive partners, friends, family, colleagues, and bosses. Because they are limited in their mindset and force you to be limited too. The saddest thing about this is that you limit your potential of actually getting the life YOU want.

Passion & Purpose owes no apology, so go get yours! Go get your dream!

With the Great Resignation looming worldwide and many leaving the corporate 9-5 lifestyle, we have to ask ourselves, what would you do if money wasn't an object. How would you be living your life? And would you be working the job you are in now? Be honest.

Create your dream life based on what you truly aspire to, no matter how unconventional it may be. Do you want to be traveling every few months and living in a different country from time to time? Do you want to be skiing in the Swiss Alps one season and chilling in the Bahamas another? Do you wish to create multiple businesses and be known for it? Or do you want to be somewhere secluded where you can develop your spirituality like Bali, Thailand, or the Philippines, and still know you have income coming in daily? Life is meant to be lived, and the possibilities are endless. But we have been limited to a life of drudgery, living day by day, trying to make ends meet, and making a decent living. Working for the next forty years at a JOB? Is this really the vision that you had for yourself?

Our job as humans is to hold on to the thoughts of what we want, make it absolutely clear in our minds what we want, and from that, we start to invoke one of the greatest laws in the Universe, and that's the law of attraction. "You become what you think about most, but you also attract what you think about most."

John Assaraf

Our paradigm has been built upon what society and this false world has imprinted onto us. So, we have built up false paradigms of success. There are CEOs who have a lot of money, but they have little time and tons of stress. But conversely, some homeless people have a lot of time but are broke. What if there was another way? What if you could have lots of freedom and lots of money?

It's time for us as leaders to start changing our paradigms and what success means. We are all defined by a different set of values, and so we have different versions of success. What one person values, another person may not. This book is not just about making a shit ton of money, stacking it all, and showing off. It's about allowing you to have financial freedom, live on YOUR terms, and create the vision YOUR way.

Our lives are only as good as our choices. And our choices are defined by a strong vision. It is only when the vision is so strong and so clear that we can make the right decisions and choices that will lead us to our path to success and freedom.

So let me ask you again. What would you do if money was of no object?

Do it NOW!

Define who you want to be.

Define what success means to you.

If I gave you $10 million… Where would you live? What kind of car would you drive? Where would you live? Beach or mountains? What size home? How many hours a day would you work? Dream business? At what age would you want financial freedom? Help your kids with college? What new hobbies would you pursue?

How would you like to be remembered?

How many millions or billions would you like to create?

What charities would you give to?

Would you help your parents?

The vision is there for those who dare to see it. I want you in this first chapter to truly stop and think. Start with the end in mind and focus on your end goal. Your thirst for success and ambition to break free from the system must be your driving factor. You must stay hungry and stay aware. Be aware of how you have been trapped in false paradigms and ways of life that are actually stopping you from living. This is how you will create your vision; this is how you will reach your goals…

And this is how you will achieve

Freedom

LAW 2 | MINDSET

"A dream written down with a date becomes a goal. A goal broken down into steps becomes a plan. A plan backed by action makes your dreams come true."

Greg Reid

L et's talk about wealth. Wealth to many people is a concept so far from their reach because they have chosen to accept their current reality as the only truth. Most, including me, were raised with limited thinking. Not knowing that true wealth is an inside job. True wealth is a shift in mindset. Will you allow yourself to be a victim to circumstance and a product of your environment? Or do you want to beat the odds and make a conscious decision to change your life today? Before one achieves greatness, one must strive to at least want to change your predetermined fate. The burning desire for yourself to want more, need more, earn more, and live more will push you to succeed.

Every person who ever reached financial freedom and ultimately success had certain qualities that forced them out of their comfort zone and into their new reality. And I am here to show you their secrets and help you find true wealth. To transform from the inside out. You must realize that wealth is a frequency. It is a pattern of continuous thinking and beliefs that turn into a way of life.

Building wealth starts with your habits and behaviors . . . your daily rituals, your ability to honor yourself, and the body, mind, and spirit you were given. It is when you realize this that things will change. There is not one person in this world that exists today (or ever) that was able to create lasting wealth if they did not have their pattern of thinking and mindset straight. That is the truth. Money will come and go. People have obtained massive amounts of money, assets and fame by sheer drive and determination. But if you don't have your mindset and energetic vibration straight, the success will not last.

"We are like magnets – like attract like. You become

AND attract what you think."

Rhonda Byrne

Making Energy into Money ⚡ 💵

Before you can become rich in money and abundant, there is one central truth you must know. Money is not absolute; energy is. Energy is the only commodity in this Universe that can create or destroy. If you wish to be abundant in every aspect of your life, choose your energy wisely. Choose the people you surround yourself with. Carefully select the books you read. Choose the place you live in, the food you eat, the things you watch, and what you listen to. If you choose drama, gossip, idle thoughts, and conversation, it leads nowhere. Not being productive, not working, and engaging in greed, vice, and sloth, you will not find yourself becoming all that you can be.

On a quantum physics level, we are all made up of sub-atoms. We are all made up of ions, minerals, and elements. How we choose to attract money and wealth is how we manipulate these sub-atoms within us. If we decide to harness the element of fire, we will indeed produce much in manifestation. But we must choose our intentions wisely. We all have the ability to manifest at speeds

17

of light, but we have been trained and indoctrinated not to do so. We all have the capacity to attract that which we desire most, but we have been trained and indoctrinated by society not to do so. We believe many aspects of our lives are not in our control because we have not yet mastered the ability to manipulate ENERGY.

Once we realize that we are the masters of our own lives, we will be truly POWERFUL. We will be able to turn matter into money; we will be able to manifest abundance. We must concentrate daily on the exact sum and amount we wish to attract. We must be intentional and purposeful with why we want this. The law of attraction is very much real. And the reasoning for this is simple.

We are all towers of manifestation because we all hold radioactive frequencies. We are like antennas, and we have enough power within us and electricity to power a city. We must remove everything weighing us down, including heavy foods, excessive meat-eating, people, noise, misinformation, friends, and things around us that fill our minds with useless energy sources. The more we surround ourselves and fill ourselves with useless energy, the more we will have to EXPEND that precious energy. So, in this sense, we must choose wisely.

We must only nourish friendships that we know will allow us to grow and elevate with positive energy and knowledge. We must only nourish our bodies with food to fuel us to carry out our day-to-day activities. We must only nourish our minds with information and things that will help us elevate on a higher frequency and level. Do not engage in sinful things that are detrimental to your growth.

You are not on the right frequency if you feel sluggish, negative, uninspired, and uncreative.

Creating An Abundance Frequency

Your energy, mindset, and the ability to put yourself first and love yourself enough to know you are entitled to more in this lifetime are what will build your wealth. It is a value, a belief system, and a pattern of thoughts and affirmations that will push you to automatically want more and, in turn, receive more from the Universe. But only when you stop limiting yourself and your potential.

I want you to know that just as much as I am, you are entitled to the endless abundance and riches that this world has to offer, but you have to believe and accept it. Believe in yourself, believe in your vision, and believe in your ability to attract and deliver everything you desire and set out to achieve. Your energy will change when you do this, your frequency will change, and your reality will also change. Change your beliefs, change your mindset, change your life.

Reframing Core Beliefs, To Change Your Current Reality

You have to forget what society thinks and forget what your family and friends think. It's time to push yourself past your limits and start living today for yourself! Too many of us have been hardwired for failure, hardwired to fall in line because we are scared of judgment. Our parents instilled these beliefs and values in many of us. We have been primed since birth and early schooling years by well-meaning teachers to mold us to what is socially acceptable, to work 9-5, to buy a house with a 30-year mortgage, have a car financed and a shit ton of student loan debt, and that is what is meant to be 'successful.'

True or false? Do you need to have a college degree to be wealthy? It's incredible how many people today would say 'true,' even though we have so much evidence to the contrary.

True or false? Do you need to be of a certain race or economic standing to become wealthy? Nope. Why would your skin color matter? Who cares how much money your parents have? Your mindset must evolve to 'if it's to be, it's up to me.' No more stories of the past. No more blame games. No more victim mentality. I'm lucky to know a lot of very successful people. This mindset is one of the things they all have in common.

True or false? Do you need to have a purpose backed by determination, grit, passion, and drive? If you said 'YES,' you are on your way to an extraordinary, wealth-filled, freedom-filled life!

I want you to stop reading right now and write down all the beliefs you constitute as 'successful.' Be honest with yourself. Identify where those core beliefs came from and who fed them to you. Was it your parents? Media? Friends? Society? I want you to think critically. Most of us have been programmed and hardwired in ways we don't know. Accepting beliefs imprinted into our minds and ways of thinking, and this forms and has shaped our reality.

Changing Your Narrative, Change Your Life

Society has predetermined core beliefs about what it means to be successful, happy, and financially independent. We must realize that there is a false narrative about how our story should unfold. Really, we should be able to write our story and create our life in whichever way we wish. Just because you didn't go to college does not mean you won't be successful. Just because you aren't married by thirty doesn't mean you are unwanted goods.

Conversely, if you've had children and gotten divorced, it does NOT mean your life is ending. It is, in fact, only the beginning. We all have the ability to be reborn time and time again in this single lifetime. As one chapter closes, another one will open. Even if you are forty now, and you feel like you have made the wrong choices in life, whether it's your partner, career path, or where you live - you can change your narrative at any given time. There are no limits. You can really choose your own adventure. No one has total control over you. There are only lessons, no mistakes. Change your narrative, change your life.

Awakening Consciousness: Becoming Aware, Making the Change

Now that you've realized you've been living in a lie, I want you to reflect on this, honestly. Becoming aware and awakening your consciousness will be the key to your new life. This is how to really change . . . You have to look at your current scenario and situation and feel so much pain and discomfort that it forces you to change. This is when transformation happens, and this is when you will be able to step into your light. Awakening consciousness is simply becoming aware of the reality that has been enforced upon you and changing it to your will. The ones determined to build a better life will be the change that this world needs to see. You should strive to be one of these people.

"Some people want it to happen, some people wish it would happen. Others make it happen."

Michael Jordan

Rising Up to the Challenge

Now for some of you, this book will only go as far as a dream that remains unfulfilled. But I sincerely hope that those who pick up this guide to wealth creation will actually take action. Rising up to the challenge of overcoming your false beliefs. Rising up to the challenge of breaking out of the 9-5 mold. Rising up to the challenge of building a business and scaling it to create a new movement, make an impact and lasting change.

We all have a part to play in this game that we call life. If you are reading this today, something has called you to realize your potential to make an impact, become a leader, and raise the collective consciousness. If you choose to move towards greatness, this book will single-handedly give you the blueprint to your freedom, wealth, and success. But you must choose to rise up to the challenge. It won't be without hurdles and obstacles because everyone who rose to success faced temporary defeat. You need to take from this chapter that you need to build the mindset, grit, and burning desire to want more, be more, and become more, and just keep fucking going! In doing so, you will give more, live more, and grow more.

Let's not waste decades of our life making corporations rich. It's time to wake up! You deserve better and should aim for better. Rise up to the challenge and make your shift from employee to becoming your own boss.

Habits & Rituals

Significant transformations and shifts start with creating new habits and building them through rituals. Habits are the foundation of lasting change. Every single successful master in this world, whoever achieved greatness, was bound by the same foundations. That is the foundation of habit. Habit is what you consistently do, which becomes automated in your daily behavior and are the building blocks to creating your new life. Your morning rituals and routine are what keep your habits together. Every micro habit that you consistently do every day becomes a daily deposit to a better future. This is the great secret. It is not the person who does one thing one time that becomes great, but the one who masters habits and forms daily rituals and routines to consistently show up, get results, and never give up.

Here are some of my daily rituals...

- I sleep at least 6-7 hours a day. Sleep is not to be overlooked.

- I drink at least 1 gallon of water a day. Keeping your body hydrated is essential.

- I get at least 30 minutes of sunlight daily. I often work in my car to force myself out of the house.

- I work out at least three times per week. I do at least 60 push-ups & 7 mins of crunches per day in the morning when I don't have time for a complete workout.

- I read or listen to audiobooks for 30 minutes a day to grow my mindset

- I watch self-improvement YouTube videos daily for 30 minutes.

- I meditate and listen to frequencies for 20 minutes daily to empower my mind.

- I manage my money & investments for at least 1 hour per day. Wealth is a priority.

- I eat or drink green foods every day. I continually flush out my body to stay lean and healthy.

Write down all of your habits and rituals. What do you eat every day? Are you fueling your body and mind for success? What do you consume on a day-to-day basis? What do you watch, read, or look at on social media? These things contribute to the 'daily deposits' in your body, mind, and spirit. Be mindful of what you consume and what you do inhabit because this will make or break your success and create the foundation of your reality.

"Excuses are the nails in the house of failure."

Collis Temple

Self-Discipline & Organization

Although habits form behaviors and rituals, discipline keeps you going to build lasting success. Pushing yourself to be consistent, disciplined, and just getting shit done will set you apart from the masses. No excuses. You must associate massive pain with not taking action and envision what would happen if you were to continue your life with the series of habits and events that you continue to do now. Is it seriously where you envision yourself in, say, five or ten years? If you know that you aren't living your best life and not truly maximizing your earning potential, you need to get disciplined - NOW. Write down an action plan each day. Show up every day, be organized, set tasks, finish those tasks, complete your goals each day, and never give up. No excuses. Self-discipline is the grit that will help you last, even when you feel like quitting. Do what others won't, so you can live a life others will only dream of.

Mental Toughness, Mental Grit

Remember, grapes must be crushed to make wine. Olives are pressed to release oil. Diamonds are formed under extreme pressure, and seeds are planted in darkness. When you feel crushed, under pressure, or in a state of darkness, you are in a powerful state of transformation. Trust the process, hold mental toughness, hold your grit. Only those willing to walk through the fire, endure the evolution and growing pains will get to the other side. They will be the ones who will build a lasting legacy and truly build lasting wealth.

The Struggle is Real

You need to understand that the struggle is part of the journey. But what defines your ultimate success and ability to grow wealth is how you deal with trials and challenges.

Remember, we are all particles of energy, negative and positive ions, atoms that turn into vibrations. We occur naturally in the essence of the environment surrounding us, which formulates our existence. But we can change that energy any time we consciously choose to.

We can mold our lives into whatever we so wish, and we can transform our entire being, reality, and physicality with genuine intention and focus. The very reason why the masses are contained is they have been stripped of the powers that enable them to transform their realities and selves. Instead, they become victims to our environment, which is an accumulation of other energies, thoughts, and perceptions that shape reality.

How funny is it that we - the most powerful living species on this planet - have reduced ourselves to automation and allowed ourselves to be controlled by external sources? When the true power lies within all of us, yet we have allowed ourselves to be molded by the external environment that exists to destroy mankind and humanity?

Let's be honest. Everyone goes through shit. What defines you and your success to get to the other side is how you deal with it. I always used the challenges to fire me up and push me harder towards the goal. The ones who go through the most pains, trials, and tribulations and overcome them are blessed to have reached the pinnacle of life lessons - allowing our pain to transform us and grow.

There is an abundance of wealth waiting for you, but we must allow ourselves to first grow, transform and shed our old self, beliefs, traumas, pains, and misfortunes. Allow yourself to take a leap of faith and follow the path and road least followed. Follow the path of YOUR dreams, visions, and ability to follow through with all the pains, woes, and trials and reach the pinnacle of growth that is the beauty we can call life. The evolution of mankind and survival of the fittest is there for the ones who can sustain the highs and lows of life and come out thriving. This is how you will grow your wealth.

It's a mindset.

It's energy.

SEE IT.

BELIEVE IT.

Then, dang it, take massive ACTION!

LAW 3 | LEADERSHIP

"A true leader always sets the standard for his people by doing it first.He never asks from his people what he hasn't already done first".

Art Williams

To become a leader, there is one thing you must do - as paradoxical as it seems, you must release control. You must remove the need for power and influence others with your frequency and energy-in-motion (emotion). You must understand how to manage the energy you emit to control the circumstances and people around you. You do not need to consciously force your opinion or position onto someone. Instead, cast the frequency. People respond naturally to the subconscious priming and thought vibrations we release.

If you are constantly in a state of panic or believe that making money and business is hard, this will become your reality. Similarly, if you think that all things happen in your favor and many are working hard to build your vision, business, and legacy, this will happen because you are emitting it in frequency. You do not need to stress out about things beyond your control. Instead, focus on the intention and goals of your outcome, and manifest it with ease.

Visualize and feel the energy within you when you are blissful from achieving these goals. Feel how others around you will feel. Nurture that feeling and cultivate success within. Feel your emotions in a state of harmony and feel yourself brimmed with joy. This sense and belief of abundance will overflow to those around you, and you will magnetize yourself. You will be harmonious in all your activities because people around you will feel your vibrant energy and a higher state of being. You cannot be dragged down by lower energy levels and negativity if your vibration is high. You will always override the negative frequencies around you. This is what it truly means to become a leader. It is influencing others on a subconscious level and state of mind.

Transforming Your Identity into a Leader

As you move into your new paradigm and shift your mindset and habits, you will see yourself transforming and moving into a new version of yourself. Do not be afraid to lose your old identity. In the death of your old identity and ego, you will transform into the leader that this world needs you to be. Your greatest success and victory in life as a leader will be to groom and develop the ones you choose to be around into the highest versions of themselves and lead your team and business into overall wealth and abundance. We all have different gifts, skills, and niche callings in which we must educate each other to develop ourselves in human potential and elevate the world. Remember, your network is your net worth. Build your network for high performance and greatness. As a twenty-one-year-old kid, I connected with the best leaders in my field, making all the difference!

Moving into Your Greatness

As you transform into the leader you are meant to be, you will become your genuine self. Every person born into this world has the capacity for greatness and the ability to access a paradigm that is an elevated version of themselves. Unfortunately, we have been hardwired in society to be limited and shun away from moving into our light. This is not an accident. This is deliberate sabotage of the system that we have been hardwired into, where we live in a matrix world full of Agent Smith's dimming our light because they don't believe in becoming great themselves.

As we said in the last chapter, you need to not give a fuck what other people say, forget what your family and friends say, and forget what the masses try to mold you to be. If they aren't where you want to be, their opinion is irrelevant. Never take advice from someone more messed up than you. Thank them gracefully but be confident in yourself and your potential and be fiercely unapologetic. It's time to step into your greatness. Don't be dimmed by the world you are in.

"When people think you're crazy, it's just because they don't have the courage to do what you're doing."

Ryan Serhant

Visualizing and Meeting Your Higher Version of Self

All successful leaders in this world had a vision. They had self-belief, faith, and they made it work. They believed in themselves firmly that they were better than their environment. This is NOT ego when you move into a higher version of yourself to leave a legacy and positively impact business, life, and society. There is one central fact we must shift our mindset into. We all hold the key to consciousness and connecting to a higher power and source that is bigger than ourselves and allowing it to guide us into becoming larger than life and serving humanity. But this only happens when we identify our potential and surrender to the path given to us in vision. The ones who become 'larger than life' believe they are crazy enough to change the world for the greater good ... and that my friend has to be you!

Change your paradigm, change your identity, change your reality, change the world. Move into your best self. Your vision will set you on your path, but your belief and grit to refuse to give up until you meet your best self will lead you into transformation.

Self Awareness | Being Authentic in Your Mission, Finding Purpose, Creating Lasting Change

Let me ask you one question. What matters to you more than money? Ask yourself why. Those are your values. Now I want to ask you, what impact do you want to make? What is your zone of genius? Passion, talent, values, and skills. Being aware of this will set you on your path and build your new identity as a leader, leading with purpose. Believe it or not, I never chased the money. I chased the winning. I chased the Dream. And you know what? For the last two decades, the money has been relentlessly pursuing me!

The sad reality is that most of mankind doesn't even know what they are doing on this earth. They wake up, roll out of bed, drink coffee and go on autopilot mode for the day, running a race that has no end, on the hamster wheel. Do you want to be one of these people? It's time to get off that hamster wheel. You need to know why you do what you do. But more importantly, you need to wake up in the morning and LOVE what you do.

Most people wake up and hate their existence, their boss, the hustle, and the grind, so they resent their family and hate their lives. Then why the fuck are they there? If you are working for minimum wage, with minimal effort and bare minimum enjoyment - quit your damn job and do something with meaning and purpose!

Wealth comes when joy and excitement come. If you are genuinely aligned with your mission and higher purpose, you will work around the clock because your burning ambition to make a difference is stronger than waiting for Fridays to drown your weekend in vices. Being authentic in your mission, purpose, and ability to make a change - and doing what you absolutely love will make you happy. And when you are truly happy, the world is your oyster. But it's up to you to become aware and make the leap to wanting to make a change and do something that excites you to become a coach, master, and game-changer in your field.

It doesn't matter if you're an IG addict, have weird hobbies, are a reiki or spiritual healer, or are doing something socially unacceptable, like being a sex therapist (personally, I think there is a great demand for this, LOL). I can guarantee you, by the end of this book, if you have mastered your hobby and you are genuinely passionate about it, you can coach and teach your mastered art and hobby, build and replicate versions of you, create an army, build passive income and an empire out of it and live in enduring wealth and freedom. There are coaches out there teaching people random shit and making a shit ton of money just by replicating the process and building up others and creating an audience and demand for it.

Being authentic to what you are genuinely passionate about and doing what you genuinely love, despite what this world tells you is acceptable - is what will get you to the other side - where the grass is greener, the sun is brighter, and the beach is sweeter. Every day will be a holiday because when you are working on what you truly love to do, you won't have to work a day! This is what real 'Wealth on The Beach' is all about.

Understanding the Laws of Energy, Karma and Intentions | Giving to Receive

When you begin to understand that everything in this world is bound by energy, you will realize and understand the laws of karma and transaction. Every single action has a reaction. This is the fundamental law and principle of human behavior and energy science. What you give, you get back tenfold. The Universe does not discriminate between good and bad. It merely just responds. It all comes down to your intentions.

Someone can carry out the same action, a leader can have the same plans. But ultimately, what result will come out of that is the underlying intentions. You can lie to others and lie to yourself, but you cannot trick or lie to the Universal pool of energy that constantly responds to your actions and intentions. If you want to cheat and lie to your people and steal from your partners and clients, you can do this - for a moment in time. You might stack money; you may have quick wins. But inevitably, the laws of karma will come back to you, and you will lose more than you won.

"In every single move you do, when you become a leader, you must understand - every single decision you make is a ripple effect in your people, your customers, clients, your

business and the legacy you leave behind. You are the energy that will create a movement and culture. "

Kasey Phoenix

The more you give, the more you will receive back. Whether it is in your energy, time, or efforts, be wary of only giving your energy and time where it will be celebrated, reciprocated, and valued. Do not give to those who seek to just keep taking from you because you must conserve your energy for what will ultimately be valued as a leader. Remember, your energy is your ultimate currency, and your time and efforts will be what builds your wealth. Only give to the people you believe will be of value to you and your business and have the same values, vision, mission, and goals. When you are truly aligned with others, great miracles will happen. Be wary of energy vampires who seek to take advantage of you.

As you transform into a leader, you will have to give others your knowledge, expertise, experience, wisdom, and guidance. Some will not value this because they are still stuck in ego and selfishness and only think of themselves. You must give yourself wholly only to those you know are in it for the same reasons as you and want to build with you. The biggest mistake I made in business was giving too much energy & time to people who didn't believe in the vision like I did. If I had it to do over, I'd focus on spending time with people in mental and physical alignment with me.

One of my mentors, Mike Sharpe, said, "you can't turn a chestnut into an oak tree." Believe in people but do not spend your life trying to make people become something they really don't want to become. How do you know if they are the right person? They are:

- **Coachable**
- **Accountable**
- **Focused**
- **Confident**
- **They have a compelling, giant dream**

Learning the Rules to Redefine the Rules

Let me ask you something. What does success look like to you? Does wearing a suit and tie mean you're successful? Does hustling and grinding every day mean you're important? Think of all the rules defining what it means to be successful and all the paradigms we have built that have shaped our reality and world. In our experience, challenging the status quo separated us from the masses. Because when you question why the fuck you are doing things, you will be able to change the rules. Learn the rules to break the rules. Understand why they have been put in place, then challenge them and ruffle feathers. This is how you will create authentic and lasting change and impact - and how you will make a movement and army. The future belongs to the risk-takers and rule-breakers.

"Win with your heart, not your head. Win on emotion, not on logic. Have a passion for what you do, no one wants a boss, everybody wants a coach."

Art Williams

Boss or a Leader? Know the Difference

Those who are natural leaders will lead to serve. They will never attempt to feel superior over another. Instead, leaders try to elevate those around them and those they love to their level of consciousness. You see, we are all connected in this Universe, and we are all united as one from the Source. Your greatest success and victory in life as a leader will be to groom and develop those you choose to be around you into their highest versions.

You must realize that in the corporate world and mentality, a boss tells people what to do. In the real world, the leader does it himself before asking others to do the same thing. Know the difference.

We have come across many 'bosses,' but they are not leaders. Just as we have come across many leaders who lead to serve and do not resonate with being a boss. The difference is the intention. You must know there is a great secret of all the greatest leaders of this world, which is the secret of servant leadership. It is the mentality of serving to truly make an impact and create an army of fiercely loyal people, with your genuine desire to build them up.

When you are so heavily invested in the well-being and elevation of your people, you will receive that energy back - and when they will honestly buy into your vision, mission, and purpose, you will not need to bark orders because you lead from the front. The greatest companies were built on the foundation of leaders inspiring their people and being actively involved in driving them to collective success.

Moving from an Employee Mentality to Leader | Leading from The Front

A title does not make you a leader. What makes you a leader is your ability to lead from the front. This book wouldn't be complete without me talking about leading from the front. Leading from the front is the most essential trait a leader must have. Let's think about it, when you're in a war or battle, your leader better be charging first! I know that most people don't have confidence when they first begin a new business or venture. They're scared. They don't know what to do. So, when I quit my job and went full-time, I had to develop a leadership mentality quickly. I asked other leaders what the most important thing I should do was? They said, personally, lead from the front.

What does that really mean? It means if I want my people to recruit, I better go recruit first. If you want your people to sell, dang it, you go show them how to sell. I would get results and then come home and call all of my key people and tell them precisely what I did and how I did it. I wasn't bragging; I was trying to inspire them. I wanted to prove that my business worked, and they could do it too. They would see that it was pretty easy. And once they knew it was easy, they would try and see that it actually worked! I think you and I would agree that success comes so much faster when you have a good leader leading you.

Shed the Ego, Win the War

Leaders learn from their people as much as they teach. They have reduced their ego because they know that they can be a master in one area of life, but the more that you know - the more you realize you don't know!

No one ever got to the next level without first shedding ego and being coachable themselves. Remember, the master was once a novice, and the leader was once a student. You must always stay humble and accept criticism and feedback when needed for the greater good and accomplishing a common goal. This is when you will understand the true meaning of being a leader and leading from the front, being the example that you wish to see in your people. You must be the inspiration of first striving for mastery yourself so that you can teach that to others.

The best high-performance coaches are the ones who have first mastered their craft and lead by ultimate example. To do this, you must be coachable yourself, accept criticism where needed, and not be afraid of failure or temporary defeat because every failure is a building block to success.

If you expect your people to go out there and hunt for business, you need to do it yourself. If you want your people to close, you show them how to close by, closing! This will inspire people to follow you, respect you and be loyal to the business and cause. Too many bosses tell their people what to do and demand respect but haven't earned true loyalty and respect. Authentic leadership is being alongside your team ready, coaching them, teaching them, inspiring them by getting results. A natural leader also takes the losses and overcomes defeat alongside their team. This is how you genuinely get people working with you - when they see you are working for them and the vision.

"True leaders are defined by their actions, not words."

Daniel Alonzo

Release the Need for Control

I never really wanted to be the boss. I just wanted to be your business partner. Maybe it's a little bit because I'm sort of an introvert. Everybody thinks I'm an extrovert because I'm loud and like to have a great time. But the truth is I like being by myself. I like being alone sometimes. So, I think building a business like mine was perfect for me because I wanted to help people, but I didn't feel like I wanted to boss them around all day long. I felt like if I built a system and taught them what to do, they could actually go do it. If they had success and then started to train their own people and teach and coach their people well, they would make money, and so would I.

I didn't really want to be in control of anyone. Believe it or not, I was never one of those coaches that would take my people to the mall and show them how I prospect in front of everybody. No one ever did that for me. I just felt like if they knew what to do, I would give them the freedom to go do it. When a coach is looking over your shoulder, I sometimes think it makes the trainee even more nervous. That's why I put together videos and systems and manuals so they can learn at their own pace. I just wanted to give them the tools to build a great business for themselves and their families, just like I did.

Remembering Why You Started | Believe in Your Contribution and Impact to The World

I started a business because I couldn't stand being told what to do. I knew I would be an entrepreneur when I played baseball in college. I remember running laps, and the coach was yelling at us. He was so angry because we had a bad game. I was thinking to myself, they're not even paying me to play baseball. If somebody's gonna yell at me, at least I want to get paid. Not too long after that, I hurt my knee and officiated basketball class, haha! My baseball career was over. Shortly after that, I went into business, and the rest is history!

"Once I commit, I'd rather die fighting than quit."

Elena Cardone

All leaders must decide that they're not gonna quit. You're not going to quit on yourself, and you're not going to quit on your people. Have an attitude of I'm gonna persist through any obstacle until the goal is obtained. A great way to never quit is to continue to self-improve. I'm talking about reading books, YouTube videos, audiobooks, seminars, you name it. When you self-improve and put in countless hours of energy and time, you will get very good at your craft and have some success. And then when you see the success, it'll give you the confidence to keep going. In the beginning, it was all about visualization and focusing on what I wanted.

I truly believed that whatever I thought about would become my reality. Some people might laugh at that, but I worked harder, got up earlier, stayed later, and beat the competition because of my deep conviction. I am a leader. I am a leader because I didn't quit. I lead from the front. I did what I said I was going to do. I always had a sense of urgency to get results. That's why people followed me. It's because they knew that I could take them to places that may be in the beginning they felt like they couldn't take themselves. Because I always showed up and was the rock, they believed me.

"I promote using bravado. I play to people's fantasies. People may not always think big themselves, but they can get very excited by those who do. That is why a little hyperbole never hurts. People want to believe that something is the biggest, the greatest, and the most spectacular."

Donald J. Trump

Another reason that people followed me was that I'm an incredible promoter. I promote my business with passion! I just believed more than most. Even though secretly I was scared sometimes, I kept going. I'm a client of all the products that I market. I practice what I preach. I'm never going to sell you anything that I don't believe in & own myself.

Big promotion means getting people to see and feel what you are selling. When you sell the dream, you must sell that person a feeling of what can be. It's a picture of their future. "What if this could happen to you?" Ask, "If this could happen to you, how would you feel?" You are dragging their dusty old dreams off and giving them a renewed spirit of excitement. Remember that most people haven't been excited about life since their childhood. The last time most people got a trophy was when they were ten.

Another thing you need to do as a leader is cultivate a competitive mindset. You need to understand that competition is fuel. A competitive environment is essential to a world-class team. Challenge your teammates to rise to the occasion. "You're not gonna let John beat you, are you?" "Did you know John just wrote a sale?" "I know you are better than where you are at." "It's time for you to step up and go for #1!"

People want to be a part of a winning team. Even though I was tough and sometimes rough around the edges, I cared about our people. I was focused on building great relationships. I'm talking about genuine relationships that were lifelong friendships. I was so young when I decided to become the leader; it was sometimes challenging because some of the people I recruited were ten, fifteen, and twenty years older than me. That's why I had to be very focused. They were watching me. They were deciding if I was the leader that could take them somewhere extraordinary. Do you know what's crazy? I never missed a meeting in twenty years. That's how consistent I was. I was the first one there and the last one to leave week after week after week after week. And you know what? I could probably count on my hands the times I was late during all those years. Leaders show up early or at the latest on time.

Another reason why they called me the leader is because I went full time. I burnt my bridges! No one ever became successful without courage and risk. Was I fearful when I quit my job and went full time? Yep. But I knew no one would take me seriously if I didn't go all in.

Let's talk about Accountability

Accountability is the #1 thing you will need to be and do as a leader. Why? Because holding people to a set of standards and goals will give them the best chance for success. When people come from a job environment, in the beginning, most will need to be gently pushed to perform. Think about it. They have been told what to do their whole life, hour by hour. So, when they go into business, some are lost. I think I was lucky because I played sports. I learned to be coachable. I learned to be accountable to a coach and a team. In the end, because I was coachable to my mentor, my teammates were coachable to me. That's pretty simple, isn't it?

You must remember that you, as the leader, are being watched. Your people are watching your actions and listening to your words. Are you positive? You see, I was the most positive! I was the most excited! 90% of winning is staying excited! Especially when things aren't going your way. Especially when things are going to shit. That's when a leader steps up and rises to the occasion with confidence, conviction, courage, determination, and passion! I think they called me the leader because I wasn't a victim. I took personal responsibility for all my actions. I decided decades ago that I would live an excuse-free life. I guess I'm just more mentally tough than most.

Got a question for you. When you fall, how fast do you get up? Do you whine and cry about problems? Or do you look for solutions to fix the challenges?

A leader is TOUGH.

A leader WINS.

Will you do what it takes to be a Leader?

LAW 4 | QUALITIES OF THE WEALTHY

"Remember, no more effort is required to aim high in life, to demand abundance and prosperity than is required to accept misery and poverty."

-Napoleon Hill

Before you can become rich in money and abundance, there is one central truth you must know. Money is not real; energy is. Energy is the only commodity in this Universe that can create or destroy wealth. If you wish to be abundant in every aspect of your life, choose wisely your energy frequency and what you absorb. Choose the people you surround yourself with. Choose the books you read. Choose the place you live in and the food you eat. Choose the things you watch and the things you listen to. Every single thing in this Universe depicts your overall success.

What you feed your mind; you will grow in fruition. So, feeding on nonsense, gossip, idle thoughts or conversation that leads nowhere, not being productive, not working, and engaging in mindless activity, vice, and sloth, you will not find yourself where you want to be, which is your highest potential.

Setting Your Frequency, Maintaining New Character

When you are building your business and your personal brand, you must realize that to succeed, you must stay on the path, setting your frequency to align to meet your new and higher self. This means maintaining your new character by building new habits, routines, people you mingle with, and what you absorb. Everything is energy. You are energy. With passion, determination, and courage, what you focus on will ultimately become your reality. So, if you want to focus on success, wealth, and financial freedom, you must carry out new aspects of your character and identity that will align with it.

Each day you must wake up, set yourself up for success, talk about success, and act successfully. It's funny, but I literally chant every morning in the shower, "I'm alive, I'm awake, and I feel great! I feel good, I feel fine, I feel this way all the time!" As I look in the mirror, I say things like, 'I'm a stud. I am a winner. I am creating the life of my dreams!"

The ones who hold integrity in this mindset will be the ones who will become truly wealthy. Wealthy people do this and have always done this. Self-talk, affirmations, and intention are the secrets to setting your frequency daily. You must design your life. Discipline, mental toughness, resilience, patience, grit, empathy, and knowing where to exert your energy will set you up for success. Nothing and no one else will do it for you.

Doing What Others Are Not Willing to Do, No Excuses

Many want success, want wealth, want freedom, and want 'the life.' But very few are willing to put in the time, energy, work, and effort to get there. Most wait for things to be handed to them or put themselves at the mercy of a corporation, government, or higher entity to control their lives and fate. Are you one of these people?

Don't allow yourself to be a victim of a system. Instead, create your own life and system. Create your life by design. It's not even about just visualizing what you wish your life was like. It's getting up and doing the fucking work! I am sorry, but anyone who believes that they can just manifest their dream life by sitting there and meditating is delusional.

There are other elements to success, which goes with taking MASSIVE ACTION. Doing what others are unwilling to do and not falling in line like sheep. If it hasn't been done, GOOD! Do it; that's a sign for you to get up and do the work to get it done.

I remember driving home one night at about 11pm from a prospective home in nearby mountains. It was raining, and shit, the roads were narrow and winding! And to top it off, I didn't make the sale. That's when I knew I would make it. Why? Because I knew most people wouldn't do what I was willing to do.

Most people would have quit because they didn't make money that day even though they worked hard. Most people just couldn't mentally handle the rejection. You see, the ones who strive for greatness don't do it just for a paycheck. Sometimes they work for free. Giving value, creating, etc. They know their payday is coming, so they persist, work hard, take the pain, so one day, people will remember their name. You must be doing what others are not willing to do because this is what will set you apart from the masses.

If your friends and family are staring you down and saying that you won't make it, GOOD. You are on the right track! The greatest entrepreneurs and people who have made a substantial impact and change in this world were big rule breakers and significant risk-takers. I've tried and failed so many times in business. Thousands of prospects have said NO to me. Not once did I ever throw in the towel and give up. You have to keep on going! I remember my friends would say so many times, let's go out, it's Friday night! I would say, I'm sorry, but I have training the next day. So instead of going out, I stayed home, creating scripts, recording tapes to teach my agents, building systems so I could duplicate my business faster and longer lasting! Do what others won't do, so you can have a future others will dream of having. Push limits. Break the rules. Do it and a little bit more.

Time is A Luxury | Using Your Time Wisely

This goes without saying that time is your most valuable asset. The time we have on this earth is limited, don't waste it living someone else's life. Don't waste your time building or working for someone else's dream or business. If you are going to waste time, waste it wisely. Every single thing you do on your journey should be working towards a goal. We all have the same twenty-four hours in a day. What you do with those hours will ultimately compound and contribute to your overall lifestyle. The daily deposits and habits that you do will accumulate your wealth. Nothing else. You must start daily habits, even if it's twenty minutes a day, meditating, writing for thirty minutes a day, exercising, reading - using micro-tasks wisely each day that will compound into success and achievements. You must realize and wake up to this… Don't waste time, or time will waste you!

Instead of wasting your time going out on meaningless expensive lunches and dinners, 'networking' events that led nowhere or hanging out with friends and family who have no direction - use your time by yourself, know yourself, get to know what you truly enjoy. This is where you will find your purpose; this is where you will find your passions. This is where you will eventually find business concepts, hobbies, and ways of generating income through novel sources. Use your time to master a skill or discipline. Use your time to master YOU. All of these things will surely pay off in the long run, which will lead you to build wealth.

Discipline | Doing What You Say You Will Do

If there is one rule that you can't ever break, it's this one.

Discipline is doing what others are unwilling to do, doing what you say you will do and sticking to it. Sticking to a schedule, a routine. Time management and organization are not wishes; they are non-negotiable. If you stay strong with your routine and schedule, eventually, you will build credibility. Whether it is in athletics, in business, or in any field. When you do what you said you would do, you strengthen your character. It is an energy; it is an attitude and a mentality that very few hold in high regard.

The most successful entrepreneurs and business owners acted with discipline to get their businesses up and running. As a business owner, you are not punching a clock for a paycheck. It's up to you to wake up on time, show up early and create value. It's up to you to put yourself through the hurdles and push through. This also goes for being disciplined in mind, body, and spirit. Are you eating right? Are you moving your body every day? The little things compound the change for the better over time.

"Commitment is doing the thing you said you would do long after the mood to do it has passed"

Ray Higdon

Consistency & Patience | It's All About Being Excitedly Patient

Rome wasn't built in a day, and no one person in this entire Universe ever achieved their dream without cultivating consistency and patience. A person's wealth is not built on one transaction or winning the lotto. Most who do get easy money lose it just as quickly. It's because they did not carry out the consistency and patience to receive it. Consistency is everything. It's posting on your social media every day. It's prospecting twenty names a day. It's making sure that you add new qualified appointments to your schedule every day. It's about getting a check a day. Results matter. Wealth is not an overnight job, just like mastering any skill. It takes months, even years, to build something that will last. That's where patience comes into play.

Throughout your whole journey, you must cultivate and practice the art of not only consistency but enduring patience. You must understand the laws of delayed gratification and begin with the end in mind. Most people want things fast and now. We live in a microwave society where anything can be given to you at a touch of a button. You can order food on Uber Eats, you can watch a video that can teach you anything on YouTube at the push of a button. But the irony in all of this is that it will never be enduring. To build a long-lasting relationship, business, or anything that will be sustainable throughout hard times requires true consistency and patience.

You will understand this parable if you have ever heard of bamboo shoots in China. It takes many years for a bamboo shoot to sprout. You can plant the seeds, and nothing will happen over seasons, regardless of you watering and nurturing it. You won't see any substantial growth. But the miracle of the bamboo shoot is that - just one day, sporadically out of nowhere, it will shoot ten feet tall. The moral of this? You must never give up and be excitedly patient in watering and planting your garden because one day when you least expect it, you will see rapid growth!

My story is similar. Got my licenses and worked hard for a couple years with little results. Then Boom! I made 100K. Then the following year, I made 250K. The year after that, I made 350K. Momentum was now on my side. That very next year, at age twenty-eight, I made 500K. And after years of investing, I saved my first million in cash!! I'm so glad I was excitedly patient and didn't give up in those early years!

Grit | Mental Toughness and Resilience

True leaders contain the fires and learn how to handle and manage them. When the going gets rough, it will show actual signs of character and grit. Those set to only ever be employees will do the bare minimum work and wait for a paycheck to arrive. The ones who can make shit happen and make money rain are the ones who can put in the energy, time, and effort, despite the hurdles and the setbacks. Most people wait for shit to happen; you have to make it happen! You must keep going despite many failures, all the

NOs, and rejections. Mental toughness and resilience are the key for those truly hungry and want to see their reality come true. Don't stop until you get the job done. And when it starts feeling uncomfortable, good. You are on the right track.

> *"Until you prove yourself, you're going to have a lot of people doubt your ability to succeed. Ignore them and believe in yourself."*

Evan Carmichael

Are you Mentally tough?

You see, I am mentally tough. You must decide to also become mentally tough. If you want to be wealthy, if you want to be a REAL leader, you can't be a cry baby, you can't be a sissy, you can't get your feelings hurt all the time, you have to be mentally capable of weathering the storms. Oh ya, there will be storms.

When you fall, how fast do you get back up? A guy I believe is the epitome of mental toughness is Hall of Fame football coach Vince Lombardi. He said that mental toughness is many things and somewhat difficult to explain, but its qualities are sacrifice and self-denial. Also, most importantly, it is combined with a perfectly disciplined will.

Did you get that? A perfectly disciplined will that refuses to give in when you know you're right. See, it's a state of mind when you're mentally tough. You could call it character in action. The next time somebody tells you something you don't like, or you experience some failure or rejection, and you just don't feel like moving forward, the mental toughness will pull you through.

And by the way, mental toughness is something that takes time to master. I've been in business for over two decades, and I can honestly say most people lack this trait called mental toughness. WHY? I believe it's a case of the 'POOR me' syndrome. If someone says something mean or coaches that person too harshly, the ego jumps in and says that's not OK!! The tone was wrong. Didn't like the facial expression. I can't allow this person to talk to me like that!

These are all of the thoughts that enter the mind. Even though the coach was right. Even though the facts were on the coach's side.

What about rejection? How do you feel about that? Does it hurt your insides when somebody tells you no way? Remember, when somebody doesn't want your product or service, it's not that they are rejecting you; they are rejecting the product or service. Therefore, never take it personally. Always spend your energy and focus on the people that want to be served.

Think about a waitress; she offers coffee to just about every person that sits down in the restaurant for breakfast. Would you say that she might ask 200 people per day, "do you want coffee?" How many of those people say yes? I don't know, maybe half? So, if 100 people told her no that day, should she feel bad? Should she quit? Should she feel hurt? Or should she just be happy that out of 200 times she asked somebody a question, half of the time they told her yes! So, if you're dealing with rejection and it's hurting your heart, just ask more people. Play the numbers.

I also see that before people go into business, generally, they are employees. Being an employee does not train you to be mentally tough. When you're an employee, they tell you what to do, tell you when to show up, tell you when to go home, and tell you what you've got to do at every level of your job. Whereas when you build a company, you have to take responsibility. You take on the risk. You get knocked out sometimes; you get beat up sometimes.

Being a leader is not always easy, but let me tell you something, it's way worth it. If you want easy street, go work for the government. Go work with the post office. But if you're going to be wealthy, you've gotta be tough as nails. You've got to believe in what you're doing, and then when somebody tries to stop you, with all your will, with all your might, you need to fucking push through! And when you do, and when you win, you're gonna feel so proud of yourself.

Lead With Integrity, Aligning Your Values with Purpose

Let me ask you something. If money were not an option, and it held no significance in what you would choose to do with your life, what would you do? Most people can't answer this question. Why? Because people chase the money. Not knowing that whatever you are passionate about will lead you to your purpose. And that purpose will lead you to the money. When you are truly integrated and aligned with your values, purpose, passion, and mission, you will be able to build and hold on to success.

You must always be doing things with integrity because we are bound by Universal laws at the end of the day. Leading with integrity is an energy, a frequency, and a path that will lead you to bigger and better things. The truly wealthy in this world have built their success and fortune and held it because they are bringing value into the world. They have created services, products, offerings, provided knowledge, wisdom, and movements that have changed and impacted the world for the better. Look at Steve Jobs or Jeff Bezos. Both had a significant purpose of changing the world. They endured ridicule and failure for many years but never strayed from their mission.

"Begin with the End in Mind" means to begin each day, task, or project with a clear vision of your desired direction and destination, and then continue by flexing your proactive muscles to make things happen. It reaffirms who you are, puts your goals in focus, and moves your ideas into the real world. "

Steven Covey

The ones who know why they started and their true purpose and 'WHY' have the advantage.

My WHY was always my family. Even before my kids were born, I was planning for my kids. I dreamed of the day when money would never have to be an object. I knew that if I built something big, I could pass on a legacy. I wanted to know if a family member needed help, I could just write a check. Kids wanted a new bike. Wife wanted a new purse; I wouldn't ever have to say NO. If my mom got sick, I could write the check for the medicine. My WHY also included proving that I could become successful at something. I believe I won because I found my mission and made it my life's work.

When you have a true purpose, knowing why you started in the first place, and feeling that sense of discomfort that pushed you on your path - that is when you are on your way. Remember the pain of having to live paycheck to paycheck; remember the discomfort of reporting to a low-life manager or a company that treated you like a number. Remember looking at those videos of people on Instagram, traveling to far-off places, living the dream. Remember not having enough money to just enjoy the finer things in life. But most of all, remember . . . After all of this - after all this fortune and wealth you will build up - the end goal was never money.

It is freedom.

This will push you to thrive, and this is why you will wake up every morning and grind like there's no tomorrow. Because you know you aren't on a hamster wheel that has no end at the end of the day. The end goal is always *FREEDOM*.

Value Experience Over Things

You can always buy more things, but you can't buy more time or re-live experiences. The truly wealthy understand this and invest in their education, experience, travel, and indulging in adventurous moments. Inevitably, they know that this is what will grow you as a person and expand your mind and bank account. Seeing how life is lived in different countries, ways, and cultures builds people to become truly successful and wealthy. Because they identify that there are different ways and lifestyles outside of the bubble they grew up in. They take time to know other people, cultures, and ways of doing things. And this translates into building your business and network.

Some of my most extraordinary adventures have brought me some of the most joy. Speaking and motivating in Canada. Elephants in Thailand. World Cup in Brazil. Safari in South Africa. Great museums in Paris. Wine tasting in Italy. Traveling around the US. Meeting new people and discovering new ways of thinking. Stuff comes and goes. Memories - this is the juice of life! Let's start squeezing!

Remembering Where You Came From | Stay Humble, But Hungry

The ones who get and stay wealthy are the ones who know humility. Because they will never forget where they came from. It's funny because I still sometimes think of myself as that short, uneducated, little Mexican kid that spent my first ten years in a not-too-good neighborhood. I think that's why I get along with so many different types of people. I remember where I come from. I never think of myself as someone better than anyone else. I can chat with a lawyer and with the gardener. I always treat them with the same amount of respect.

When I talk to a new recruit, I routinely tell them, "I work for you. I'm not your boss. My job here is to help you get every dream you desire from our business. We are going to do great things together!" I'd say things like, "With your credibility and my knowledge, there is no way you will fail. I got your back all the way!"

Never let your success get to your head. You are not as important as anyone else. Everyone has an equal amount of potential and value. A nasty ego will bring you down faster than anything. The ego keeps us from elevating ourselves to further heights because it stops us from showing empathy and understanding what our team or people around us are going through. Where you have mastered one skill, you are still a novice in another. Always be open to feedback, and always remember that every person, place, experience, or thing put in your existence and life is a chance for you to learn and grow.

"Humility is the definition of longevity."

Gary Vaynerchuk

Focus On Continuous Self Improvement

The true purpose of pursuing wealth begins and ends with self-improvement. Wanna be happier? Seek progress, not perfection. Seek growth. The person you become at the peak of your life's journey will determine your overall wealth. Your second life will begin after you realize that your past failures, lessons, obstacles, and setbacks were there to push you to grow. Your life will change when you take power in your own hands to mold and create your destiny.

The people who focus on continuous self-improvement and focus on becoming more remarkable than they were yesterday are the happiest and ultimately the wealthiest. Concentrating on all ways to grow mentally, spiritually, physically will, in turn, lead to growing financially. Those mind muscles and micro habits in self-development will trickle down into your desire to prosper and eventually align and connect with others on the same mindset and wavelength.

Progress is embedded in our DNA to adapt, evolve and grow. This desire to make life better and live as higher beings and consciousness is the natural desire of every single human born into existence. If you are not growing, you are dying. These are the natural laws of the Universe.

"The biggest mistake most people make is how they let circumstances dictate their attitude. If things go well, they have a good attitude. If it doesn't, their attitude is terrible. They start thinking badly. When things are going well, it's OK to go with the flow. But when they are going badly, you need the discipline to control your thoughts and think only about how you want things to go."

Hector LaMarque

Automate Your Life

Automating your life from your bills to your credit card payments and creating morning routines and habits will significantly change your life. The wealthy know this because they know 'time is money.' When you value your time, you will understand how much of a time-waster admin tasks and day-to-day activities are and can zap your energy. Little things that can be automated, from what you wear to what you do in the morning and evening and managing your bills can literally transform your life.

I wear lots of white, black and blue. I wear white, black and blue shoes. WHY? Because I don't want to waste lots of time figuring out what to wear. Everything matches in my closet. I don't go to the gym. WHY? Because it takes time to drive from my home and back. I work out at home. I have a one-hour routine that makes me feel great. I even do VR boxing! Less blood. LOL. I do meetings on Zoom, so I don't have to be in traffic. This saves me hundreds of hours per year. Why did I build manuals and record videos of my business-building process early in my career? So, I wouldn't have to constantly repeat myself with new recruits.

We will talk more about this later in the book. Building systems that give you back time allow you to do the things you want to do when you want to do them.

"Have a real Detox plan- Consistently helping your body clear toxins and waste material from your major organs and blood supply is critical to a healthy you! Health is energy."

Cynthia Stopani

Health = Wealth

What's the point of getting rich if you're gonna die of an illness at an early age? Years ago, I watched this movie on Netflix called *Fat, Sick, and Nearly Dead.* The documentary tells the story of how a guy lost almost one hundred pounds and healed his autoimmune disease by following a sixty-day green juice fast. It was horrifying to see this man, Joe Cross, who was so successful monetarily but dying of so many health complications.

After watching that movie, I thought I gotta take care of myself. Although I've been very fortunate to not have any medical issues or challenges, I decided that I would put health as a top priority in my life. The first thing I did was buy a super blender. I began to blend green drinks about three times per week. Here's my simple recipe: kale, spinach, cucumber, lemon, ginger root and green apple. Blend it with some water and you're on your way! My health is so important to me. I refuse to be tired and uninspired because of poor health. I rarely get sick. I've always been that dad who gets on the kids' rides. Run around with them. Play baseball, basketball and soccer. I love to hike. I love to go biking. I love snorkeling and adventure.

Did you know that when someone gets cancer, most will recommend that person get on an all-green diet? Why? Well, maybe it's because greens are filled with oxygen. And it's said that cancer cannot survive in oxygen-enriched environments. I'm not a doctor, but I figured that if I slammed my body with greens every day, I just might avoid that cancer thing.

STRESS

Are you stressed out all the time? If you are, it's time to take a check-up from the neck up. Stress is a killer. To help lower my stress, I listen to frequencies at Soaak.com each morning. It's only a 20-minute process, and wow, it centers me for the day ahead. Some studies even show that meditation promotes gamma wave activity in the brain. These brain waves are associated with focus, problem solving and even happiness. Check this out... After 60 days of meditating on wealth and prosperity frequencies daily, that following month I had the best total cashflow month of my life!

Start today to get a real plan to get your health right.

Your wealth is counting on it!

Sign up for the Soaak app experience and use code DA50 for 50% off! Don't forget to check out my 21-day program.

It's me & you for 21 days :)

LAW 5 |MASTERING YOUR CRAFT

"You are an uncut gemstone of priceless value. Cut and polish your potential with knowledge, skills and service and you will be in great demand throughout your life."

Denis Waitley

Have you ever heard of the saying 'jack of all trades, expert at none?' This goes without saying; those who dabble in many different fields and never define themselves in one set niche will never see the fruits of their hard labor.

Think about this, if you want to build a house, you can't go half in on what color to paint the walls and leave it half-finished, then start putting wallpaper on a different wall because that also looks good to you. It would look pretty shitty. You would have a half-assed home that would appeal to no one. The same goes for your line of work, career, or business concept. None of the great athletes, artists, and entrepreneurs ever achieved greatness or reaped the rewards of mass wealth without first mastering their craft. When you become a master of your field and perfect it, to the point where it can be presented to the world in its final format, you will be able to make money from it. This is a truly Universal law.

Immerse Yourself in Your Passions

Passions equal profit. Know what you are drawn to and immerse yourself in it one hundred and ten percent.

I never really felt like I was working because I was so obsessed with my business. Most people live just to work and make ends meet. They seem to get excited about clocking out at 5pm sharp. It's because it's not what they are genuinely passionate about. When you are working a 9-5, you are not working for a purpose or to fulfill your inherent desires; you are working to make a paycheck. I know this sounds ironic, but money will come when you find your purpose and passions.

Money and mass wealth do not come as a result of you working a 9-5 day of drudgery because you simply won't be inspired. You won't be inspired to do more, be more, or achieve more. If you are working hard, make sure you work hard for your passions. It's not so much what you make at the end of the day that will be of true value, but what you learn, develop in skillset, and master that will become INVALUABLE and your true asset. That is something that can never be taken away from you and can never be replaced.

When you work in Corporate America, you are a mere number that can be replicated and replaced at any given time. Working for yourself and working on your skills and knowledge will turn into lasting wealth. This knowledge and skillset can be converted into a physical gold mine if you put in the work to bring it to the masses in service or products. As Robert Greene stated, "you must discover your calling - that is your life's task." When you are genuinely passionate about your field, you will have a solid connection for wanting to master the craft, master your skills and master the discipline.

"Know what you're drawn to and immerse yourself in it."

Robert Greene

Mastering Knowledge, Skills & the Discipline

To be truly abundant and achieve solid foundations for wealth, you must master knowledge, skill, and discipline. Before creating any business, you must set the foundation of what you want to be known for and what you want to sell. Listen, as Grant Cardone said, "everything in life is a sale, and everything you want is commission." So, if you are going to sell something and make a living out of it, it has to be something you are so passionate about. You want to know every single aspect of it.

Applied knowledge is power. Whether it is a product or service, you must be specialized, and you need to know your shit! It's not enough to have an interest. If you genuinely want to build an empire from nothing, the key is mastering all fundamentals of your business. A keen knowledge of that business is the steppingstone for creating something unique, and action is the key to carrying out your dream. If you see any of the greatest athletes, artists, business moguls, coaches, entrepreneurs, and public figures, you will find one strong common thread: their ability to master their craft.

Looking back, the first thing I did when starting in business was to find out what the absolute basic fundamentals were. For example, I needed to learn how to recruit. I needed to know how to sell. Every day I practiced how to overcome objections that my future prospects would give me. I rehearsed my presentation hundreds of times by myself while going on countless presentations with actual clients to solidify my new skills.

I love baseball. It was a sport that I played when I was a kid. I remember watching the greats hit hundreds and hundreds of balls every day to get great at their sport. Blisters on their hands!! An achy body!! All to become a master. You see, everybody wants to be one of the greats. Everybody wants to be admired for what they do. Everybody wants success and fame. Most just won't put in the time or the effort to really get phenomenal at what they do. So, as you make your way into the business world, or the sports world, or the photography world, or the social media world, or the fashion world, or whatever world you are going into, just ask yourself… do you love what you're doing, and are you willing to put in the extra hours, days, months and years of massive amounts of practice effort and commitment?

If the answer is no, it will be a rough road ahead for you. If your answer is a resounding yes, get ready for a great life!

"Excellence is not given, inherited or accidental.

Excellence is earned."

Brad Lea

Defining Your Niche

In a time where we live in an information age and technology-driven world, the amount of information accessible to us at the touch of a button has never been greater. However, we have also found a new problem in providing trustworthy and reliable business service and expertise.

Everyone wants to be seen as the expert in their field, but to truly become an expert in your craft, you must identify what you have that other people don't. This is where having a unique selling proposition comes into play. A unique selling proposition or USP is the point of difference you have in the market that stands you out from the rest. For example, if you are going to be an expert in financial services, what type of services would you fall in? Are you a broker that sells home loans or commercial loans?

If you are in recruitment, what kind of industry and roles are you recruiting? If you are an influencer, what are you selling and promoting - lifestyle, beauty, business, or fitness? Also, if you are an artist, what type of music or art is your genre. Whether you are a medical practitioner or an HR Manager, the ones who are heavily focused on defining their niche are the ones who get paid the BIG BUCKS. You have doctors who earn okay money, working as a generalist in medicine, but the ones who reap the real rewards are the surgeons and medical specialists.

Take Kasey, for example. For years in Corporate Australia, she worked as an HR generalist. Working across all aspects of HR in some of the largest banks and corporations. From recruitment and performance management to termination, employment law, training, and development. She became extremely burnt out. It wasn't until she took the leap building her own recruitment agency as a corporate headhunter that she specifically homed in and niched down in recruiting. She focused on investment bankers, lenders, brokers, and executives in the banks and Australia's financial and broker firms, truly defining her niche. This was when she made it rain. From working a whole year as an HR Manager and Recruitment Consultant earning six figures to suddenly making six figures in one month!

This is the power of niching down. When you are so specialized in your craft, you no longer need to sell your services because you define your services in that field just by specialization alone. The business will come to you because you are the 'go-to' guru!

The more defined your niche is, the more specific your target market and the audience will be. The more detailed your target market will be - the more specific your consumers and buying clients will be because this is what you will be known for in your industry. The easier it will be for you to develop your knowledge and skills to perfect your offerings - because you are honing your craft.

Do it NOW!

Make a point right now and write down what you feel like you bring to the table and how you can define your niche in your industry, interest, or field of expertise.

What is your industry?

What are your key skill sets?

What do you want to be known for?

What do you feel would be accessible in promoting or selling, in terms of service or product offerings?

Who is your desired audience and target market?

"The longer you hang in there, the greater the chance that something will happen in your favor. No matter how hard it seems, the longer you persist, the more likely your success."

Jack Canfield

Finding a Mentor, Replicating Their Moves

When you get genuinely immersed in a discipline or a field - whatever it is, finance, brokering, hairdressing, reiki healing, beauty, or fitness - you will find someone, somewhere in the world, in some space in time, that has achieved the greatness and the fortune that you are seeking. You must strive to emulate their actions and research precisely how they have excelled in becoming successful. This is the fastest route to becoming wealthy, and this is the surest way to find success in your field.

I can guarantee you that there are people online who have made a killing out of photography, built courses, replicated the process, and made a shit ton of money selling it online. There are fitness moguls who have packaged up their skills, knowledge, and expertise and put it in an app. There are reiki and spiritual healers who have mastered their craft and been able to teach this to others and build courses to pass on the wealth of knowledge and charge thousands of dollars for their wisdom.

Some people found a service or product, sold it & made millions! It doesn't matter what discipline you are in - I want to show you how to make your passion and purpose into a business and how to build it into something that can be replicated by sharing your skillset. You just need to be able to tap into the right networks and find the right people to facilitate your growth, knowledge, and expertise in that field so you can pass this on in the business. Find inspiration from your heroes, find others that push you to become great.

The first time I met my mentor, he wore a bright red jacket in a little restaurant that I used to frequent. His name was Hector

LaMarque, and at that time, twenty years ago, he was making over a million dollars a year in passive income. That would be like someone earning $1.8 million in today's dollars. To me, a twenty-one-year-old making seven dollars an hour, a million dollars a year was pretty sensational, for lack of a better word. I thought to myself, 'wow, if I could just make $100,000 a year, I'd be the happiest person on the planet.' So, my training began.

I told my mentor that as long as it was legal, ethical, and moral, there was nothing that I wouldn't do. I was a 'whatever it takes' kinda guy! I told him as long as he didn't lie to me, I would always be loyal, and I would always work my ass off. I didn't care how many hours I had to work. I didn't care what task I had to perform. I was willing to go all in and do what needed to be done so that I could have his kind of life. It took me a couple of years of training until I started figuring things out.

I'd never worked in sales before. I'd never led anything or run a company before. So, I knew that I had to be patiently excited. I was so excited every day to learn new things. Of course, I got frustrated when I took on rejection. It wasn't always easy. As a matter of fact, it was frustrating as hell those first few years. But you know what, I never wanted to quit. All my goals were written down, and I kept thinking, what will I do if I quit? If I gave up, none of my goals and dreams would come true. A job wasn't going to give me a dream home. A job wasn't going to provide me with the car of my dreams. A nine to five job sure as hell would not allow me to travel to far-off places and have tremendous freedom to do what I wanted to do whenever possible! So why would I quit when things got hard? I knew that eventually, I'd figure this shit out. I would make progress, and if I followed my coach, I'd start winning.

Engaging a Coach

That is when I found the importance of engaging a coach. I called my coach every single day for five years. So, what if it took me a couple years to figure it out. By the way, within those couple of years, the coaching was pretty tough. I didn't always like what he told me. Was he always Mr. Nice guy? No way! He used to challenge me every day - just to get me to compete. He hurt my feelings sometimes. I didn't care because it was just making me more mentally tough. That is where real growth happens.

When I would say the wrong thing in a presentation, he would tell me the right way to do it so that I would have better results the next time. This built my mental agility and resilience. I didn't want my coach to be nice all the time. I wanted him to tell me the things that I needed to hear, not just what I wanted to hear. That's why I got so good so fast. That's why my business exploded, and my income exploded. I did the right things with my money, and I woke up at twenty-eight, as I've told you before, financially free. Do you have a coach? If you don't, you need to decide right now to find one today.

"When you buy knowledge, you buy time. Learning is the only way to buy down the time tax of ignorance."

Alex Hormozi

Finding and Investing in a Coach

You might be thinking, but I don't have a coach. How the heck do I find a coach, and how the heck do I know that they're going to be any good? As you know, there are a lot of people online today.

They make a lot of promises. Will they deliver for you? Here are a couple of things that you should look for in a great coach:

- **Are they having the success that you desire?**
- **Are they willing to hold you accountable?**
- **Do they have a vested interest in you?**
- **Do you have a good connection?**
- **Are they a true expert in their field?**
- **Do their testimonials check out favorably?**
- **How long have they been in business?**

Once you identify these in your chosen person and create a strong connection, you will know they are the one that will bring you to manifest the life and success you desire.

So, you found a coach. Now here's my advice: build a strong relationship with that person. Be coachable, of course, but really get them to like you and trust you. This is a contact and a relationship that you can foster for years and years and years. Who knows, maybe you become the best of friends and they even give you opportunities that you didn't even know existed in the future.

You never want to treat your mentors with disdain because you might need them one day. Don't burn that bridge because you got mad at your coach. I can tell you I didn't always like my coach. Many times, I disagreed with his opinion. But I kept my mouth shut because I respected him very deeply. He was making more money than I was. Who am I to tell him I disagreed? He's a wise man. He was an expert. He had a vested interest for me to be successful. He was in business for over twelve years when I started. And I knew I wanted to keep that relationship no matter what. Now, twenty-five years later, we are the best of friends. He has, through the years, always offered advice and still continues to help me when I need it to this day.

Now that you know the importance of specializing your knowledge and finding mentors and a coach to bring you to the next level, you will realize that the most important thing after all this - is finding the right networks.

Because your network is your net worth.

LAW 6 | YOUR NETWORK IS YOUR NET WORTH

BUILDING YOUR NETWORK

"You will never outperform your inner circle."

John Wooden

Your network is your total net worth. You are the sum total of your influential inner circle because energy is currency, as you have already gathered. What you emit, you will receive, and that will be in the connections you build and the network you develop. When you are at your lowest point or have lost everything, you will be able to bounce back and build a business and transact goods and services in whatever your domain is, just by having a solid network.

However, you must know that when you move into your new paradigm and identity, you will naturally lose some people in your life, whether friends or family, because they are no longer aligned to your newly elevated energy and path.

The rudest awakening in your growth, though - will be the strangers in your life that connect with your work and what you stand for - they will buy your products, engage in your services, and vouch for you - rather than the people in your previous relationships and former social circle. Your old life, and the friends and family you have come to know, unfortunately for most, will not understand your new path.

They won't buy your products or services, and most of the time will ask for handouts or freebies because they are 'friends.' Be cautious of these people in your life because they will drag you down to lower vibrations and zap your newfound energy and momentum.

Do not be afraid of shedding old skin and relationships.

It is not a case of thinking you are better than others, but a case of understanding that you are no longer in alignment with them and are on a different path. When you know this, you will make peace with it, and you will learn to shed and evolve from relationships in a healthy manner. This is the transformation process in which you align with higher vibrational people who are more in line with your mission, life purpose, and where you are going. Where one door closes, another opens. Start building a new network of like-minded people and individuals. Create an inner circle, build a community. Connect with other leaders in your field where you can draw from the same audience and customer base. Find a coach, be a coach. Build your empire through the people around you.

Create a Strong Inner Circle

They say your success is the sum of the five to seven people in your inner circle and who you hang with the most. It's the truth. When you are around others, you share energy, thoughts, and vibrations. You share a way of thinking, a way of life. Be careful with whom you allow in your inner circle. I was forced to do this early on in my life. I had to tell my best friends that I grew up with I'm moving on. Not because I didn't love them. Not because I was better than them. Not because they were bad people. I knew that those people would not bring value to my mission. Every time they wanted to take me away from my focus, I slowly lost steam. Some of them were so negative.

I had a best friend named Adam. Adam told me I wasn't smart enough to make it. My new business was a scam; I needed to quit my business, go to college, and get a good job with benefits. I told him to just be supportive as a friend, and we could stay friends. He decided to continue his negativity, so I drew a line in the sand, and we went our separate ways. I hope Adam is reading this because, believe it or not, he changed my life! When I cut off the relationship, it pushed me to prove to him and my doubters that I could make it. In the end, I lost friendships but gained so many others. If I had stayed in my little circle, never taken a risk, I wouldn't be writing these pages today.

Make sure whoever you engage with daily adds as much value and elevates your energy as you are to them because everything in life is a transaction. Whenever you engage with any person, you are transacting in energy exchange. Whether it is someone at the coffee shop while you buy your morning coffee to the people you work with or do business with daily. You are sharing energy and thought vibrations. Once you realize this, you will learn to value your power as a true form of currency exchange.

Think about this. Suppose you are engaging with someone of low vibration, with a negative mindset, constantly complaining about life, attracting negative circumstances, and having a 'can't do it' attitude. What do you think will happen to you? Who the fuck wants to be around negative Nancy and people who constantly say, 'it can't be done?'

This attitude, mindset, and view towards life will rub off and also become you! It's not about being perfect or better than others; it's about aligning with the right vibrations that will push you up to an elevated version of yourself, constantly improving and not lowering your vibration. If you feel anxious or have a strong intuition about someone being off around you, chances are, it's true! Your gut knows more than you! This is the Universe, and your energy vibrations tell you that this person is not aligned with you - cut that bitch off!

Master Talking to Strangers & Aligning with the Right Vibration

Now that you know how to weed out the bad eggs around you and those who are not aligned with you and your path, you need to realign and find people who are! You must become aware and put your antennas out to match others on the same wavelength, mindset, and vibration. You will know when you are aligned because the people you connect with - will have the same views, thoughts, and perspectives.

During your building process, it is crucial in this stage of your transformation that you only connect with people who will seek to help you in business and in life and desire to grow together. Sharing knowledge, ideas, wisdom, ways of operating, and values are among the greatest ways you can master talking to strangers and building rapport. Seek to connect with others in similar groups and whatever niche or industry you are in.

Build great relationships with great people.

Building New Relationships

When you are coming up in your new domain or your business niche - you need two things to survive and thrive. A network to vouch for you and refer your business and relationships to help you level up your discipline and skills and help you master your field. You need visibility.

> *"The quality of your life is the quality of your relationships."*
>
> **Anthony Robbins**

Aligning Your Values, Finding Your People

You will realize that not all people you come across will be directly aligned with your values on your journey. You need to be conscious and aware of this to weed out the people in your life that add no value and nurture the ones who do. Everything is energy. You must identify how you feel and respond to those around you.

If you are misaligned, there will be constant disagreements, conflict, and miscommunication. This is simply because that person you are engaging with does not hold the same values in life, the same mindset, or principles. You may be focused on building an empire, for example, to create mass impact and wealth and bring your business to the forefront of expansion. However, your business partner may just be focused on the next deal and concentrate on the dollar value to make money for themselves. You will constantly be in a state of disagreement and disharmony because you may want to keep all the funds in your business. In contrast, your partner will want continual payouts and dividends and 'expense' everything on the company.

What is going to happen?

Your business will never grow because your capital and the bottom line are not growing. You won't have enough money or revenue to scale, and you will always be scrambling for revenue to come in each month. When you are not aligned on the same vision, value, goals, and mission, your business can never thrive, and you will not be able to scale.

This even goes for personal relationships and marriages. You need to be serious about who you go into partnership with, who you choose to share your business and finances with, and who you are 'getting into bed with.' Everything is an exchange, and we all operate through alignment of frequency. If you hold the same frequency as your partner, you will watch your business and finances thrive and build wealth rapidly. Amazing things will happen when two people are focused on the same goals and put in the same amount of effort, energy, and focus.

Remember, everything is a vibration. We are all connected through a matrix of atoms, ions, and energetic frequency. So, when we are completely aligned with one another, we will surely grow and thrive in abundance, wealth, and prosperity. This is Universal law.

Strengthening Connections

As you grow further in business, you will realize the best entrepreneurs in the game know it is ABSOLUTELY A RELATIONSHIP GAME! It's not about what you know. It's about who you know and how you nurture these relationships. It's not about the degrees you have accumulated or what you have studied that will build you great wealth, but that is only one aspect. The rest is all about networking, building relationships, and being around people who can either build your business for you or are the connections. Whether they are clients, contractors, employees, or new recruits.

When recruiting people in our business, the first thing to do is to ask, what's your network like? Who do you know? Who can we go see to help get your business off the ground? I always teach our teammates to look for centers of influence. Those are people that know a lot of people. These are what we call connectors. In today's world, those people have big followers on social media. They are community and business leaders. Last year, I recruited Kevin, who had 80K followers on his Instagram. When he asked people for help, what do you think they said? Yes. Of course. Come on over. Yes, I'll book a Zoom call. He was wildly successful! You see, when you build with influencers, business is fun and easy. But how do I meet these people? First, push yourself to become a person of value to create a connection. Once a connection is built, the relationship can be formed.

"You can make more friends in two months by becoming interested in other people than you can in two years by trying to get other people interested in you."

Dale Carnegie

Expanding Your Network

Your ability to build solid networks and relationships will bring you to your wealth. Find referral partners and people that will vouch for you, root for you, and share your work with others. This is why the saying goes, 'your network is your net worth.' You are the sum of the people you surround yourself with.

Be vigilant in who you share your space, time, and energy with. Keep expanding by meeting new people and making new friends. Sure, some will disappoint you, but you must keep moving forward. Every contact is energy that can lead to future opportunities. Always be on the lookout for great people. People that are motivated. People who are people of value and substance. When you are invited to a party, go. Ask questions and get curious about others. Smile. Be sincere with praise. Laugh and have fun. To be remembered is to be memorable.

Maintaining Social Grace in All Your Interactions

The wealthy do not look down on others with less. Real leaders seek to lift those around them. This is a must. Social skills are increasingly important on your way to success and wealth. Understand that the true value is not just about your success but how you can elevate others. This is the importance of 'social eloquence.' Be discreet in your social interactions and stay classy and emotionally calm in the face of adversity. Value the people around you and those not aligned with your path anymore - disconnect gracefully and wish them well.

When someone quit on me, I always tried to salvage the relationship. Don't waste your time and energy in drama, conflict, or pushing your views on other people. The ones who aren't aligned with your vision, mission, or purpose are on a different path. To know this is to win. Because you are keeping your energy focused on what is important to you.

Becoming Emotionally Intelligent

Elevate Yourself. Your Network is Your Net Worth.

Bottom line, if your relationships don't push you or elevate you to become a better version of yourself, you need to cut it off. Conversely, you will know, if someone has been put in your life and you have grown in money, knowledge, character, and mindset, you know they are good for you. If you are around a bunch of friends that talk gossip, live for the weekend, and live paycheck to paycheck - guess what - that will become your reality because you allow them to prime your subconscious for that reality, and you will find yourself living an identical life. But if you choose to connect with like-minded people who like to talk about ideas, know how to build wealth, and connect each other for business opportunities, guess what. Eventually, you will meet the same success.

Everything is energy, and everything is an energetic transaction. We must be mindful of who we are putting our time and energy into because energy is the ultimate currency. Your net worth will ultimately be depicted from your network. That's just the way life is. You must strengthen your connections with the network you know will be of equal value. Be mindful of how your energy responds to others; intuition does not lie. So, if you feel like someone is not right in your inner circle, most likely, this is your intuition telling you that you are not aligned. Always stay on the path and be focused, and the Universe will align you with the right people that will help you reach your goals.

"I don't give so I can get, I get so I can give."

David Meltzer

Sharing Your Wealth

There is no point in having the blessings of this world when you don't have people in your inner circle to share the abundance around you. Make sure you build a solid network that aligns with your higher self and will facilitate your growth to the fullest potential on your rise up. Mentally, physically, spiritually, and financially. This will be a crucial concept to your transformation and evolution to wealth.

Say Thank You

Would you like to truly make more friends and build more lasting relationships? Here's how. Say thank you. Say thank you when somebody does something small for you and say thank you when somebody does something big for you. Say thank you for being my friend. Say thank you for having my back. Say thank you for making me smile. Say thank you for holding the door for me. Say thank you for being such a nice person. Do you really wanna be happy? Here is how. Say thank you to as many people every day as you can. Saying thank you will bring you more joy and bring the world more joy!

Say I'm Sorry

My daughter Ava, (age 16, new driver) just hit the gate in front of our home. Literally, like, a few hours ago! I'm gonna be honest, it scared me and I kinda of lost it. I was rude and not very loving in that moment. I just deeply apologized to her a few moments ago. I said, "Ava, I'm so sorry for not being more loving and supportive this morning. I was upset and did not respond the way I should have. I want you to understand that I love you and I'm not angry with you. I know your feelings were hurt today and I'm really sorry." Whether it's your family or a teammate, when you make a mistake, own up fast, take responsibility and then move on.

That's what leaders do.

LAW 7 | LIFTING PEOPLE UP

"Great leaders make you feel important."

John Addison

The Roman empire was not built by one man. Apple did not become a trillion-dollar empire by Steve Jobs alone. Even the most significant artists, athletes, entrepreneurs, and thought leaders had mentors who built them to what they are today and lifted them up because they BELIEVED IN THEM. This is the secret to long-lasting success. It is the ability to build up your crew, BUILD new leaders and LIFT PEOPLE UP. Why? Because all of the most remarkable businessmen and women of this world know that to truly become wealthy, financially free, AND time free is to build leaders.

For example, when I met Kasey, I knew she had the enormous potential to build her recruitment and consulting business to something great. This was a woman I met at first glance and asked her in our first interaction, "how'd you get so fucking smart." I wasn't joking either. She has a master's degree in psychology. She knew everything from quantum physics, the law of attraction, spirituality, employment law, HR, and business. She had helped build startups for other people and recruited for some of the world's biggest banks, finance, and broker firms. But she was time poor.

She was a single mother hustling and working to build other people's businesses while managing her own different companies. All the while having her recruitment business, coaching business, online business ventures, and writing/blogging. Although it was significant and quite impressive that she had so much tenacity and drive, I told her - there is so much more money and freedom you can have once you learn how to build new leaders in your businesses and coach and mentor people to work with you instead of being a lone ranger.

She said to me, "Daniel, I wish I could, but I am so OCD, I dread the thought of teaching people things and not being in control."

That is the biggest mistake most people make. It's the fear of teaching others and lifting people up because ego takes control. Stamp this in your brain . . .

"Your ego will keep you broke. Your ego is the enemy."

Daniel Alonzo

The ego will keep you working around the clock and working like a hamster on a wheel and strip you of financial and time freedom. Because your ego will say, 'Hey you, no one can do your job better than you, you should work twelve hours a day instead of recruiting others, outsourcing, or delegating to someone else. No one is as smart as you.' That is the greatest trap that will keep you down, time-poor, and not maximizing your earning potential. Some people have lots of money, but they have little time. Some people have a lot of time but little money. Why?

Because they are too damn scared of sharing their wealth of knowledge with others, not knowing this knowledge passed onto others is the true answer to the test!!!

Read that again.

If you have built up a foundation of mastering your skills, knowledge, industry expertise, you have a DUTY to share that and build others up and mentor them. You have a DUTY to mankind to spread the seed of consciousness and lift people up. That's what we are here to do. To master ourselves, so we can teach others and help humanity evolve. Lifting people will be your most significant return on investment, alongside mastering yourself. Because when you do this, you are creating the foundation of building leaders in your business and the inner circle who will be able to help build your vision into reality.

Fast forward six months after I started coaching Kasey on how to build and scale her business; she partnered and mentored a young HR and Fintech Executive under her wing to run and develop her recruitment firm with her. In a short three months, she started making $100,000 a month, which is what she was previously making as base salary incorporate. Every single deal that Kasey's firm closes, she gets 50% of it, and her consultants get 50%. She is making money in her sleep.

Their firm is one of the fastest scaling recruitment firms in Australia. She has consultants working for her in four different countries with an outsourced business unit in Manila. All because she took this one piece of advice from me and built other people to work with her in her business. She mentored them, coached them, befriended them, taught them the industry process, and gave them the confidence boost to become great on their own - and also find financial freedom. This is the magic of lifting people up!

Here's another example of how building leaders can create a lifetime of recurring income. About fourteen years ago, I took over another business in our industry. Along with that business, I met a guy named Chuck. Chuck was very talented. Chuck was one of the best salespeople that I had ever met. The challenge? Chuck wasn't making very much money. I promised Chuck that if he followed my process and the game plan that I laid out, he would transform his business and one day create a multi-million-dollar operation.

The first step was to start replicating himself and helping other people become as good as him. The best and fastest way to do this in our business is to grow your big events. A big event is just a large seminar that we would hold from time to time to generate large amounts of recruits and showcase the incredible success of our business. So, I told Chuck to sell out this event, and great things will start to happen to his business. His first reaction was, no way am I going to spend a bunch of money to try to get a bunch of people to an event. I make OK money now, and I've never really had to do that before. So, count me out!

This was so important to me that I asked him and his wife to meet me at a local restaurant for breakfast. I did my best to get them to see that we could gain some traction when he got his small team to this event and got them to compete and be recognized and feel good. It wasn't easy, but Chuck reluctantly agreed to go along with my plan. He sold out to the event! His entire team showed up, and they started recruiting like crazy. They won trophies. They felt great! And in that crowd was a guy named Roger.

Because CHUCK had sold out the event, Roger got recruited and was fired up! Roger became one of the number one new recruits of the year in the entire company! He helped CHUCK build one of the most prominent offices in the world! And as they say, the rest is history. CHUCK and his wife Rita today are entirely financially independent. They run one of the top organizations in the world of financial services. Chuck not only lifted his people to win but helped them to duplicate that feeling and process. He was always the first one to sell out to every big event throughout the years. What a leader. What a champion!

"Always Treat People Good…When you're building a business like ours you got to treat people good. This is a dang volunteer army! If you don't treat them good, somebody else will."

Art Williams

Why Get Positive?

Some of you may be thinking, well, shit, that's a lot of time out of my day, and I just don't have the energy or patience for it. But what you don't realize is that lifting people up is an energetic exchange. It's a mindset; it's the act of motivating people and believing in someone. It's taking on the emotional load. It's the one kind gesture or spoken word you give to another person, whether the janitor cleaning your office toilet or your barista. You never know who you are talking to.

When you believe in people, I mean really believe in people anything is possible. Most people have such low self-esteem. Every time they think about doing something great, they get stopped in their tracks because of negative, gross thinking. Did you tell someone you believed in them today?

We all can get a negative attitude, wasting time and energy in fear and worry. Why not make the most of life no matter the stresses and challenges that come our way? You can do that by changing your focus and thinking. Cultivate a positive mental attitude, and you'll feel more energized and more peaceful when things don't go your way. Stress levels might rise when things don't go the way you would like them to, so let's talk about stress and how to deal with it.

3 Stress-Relieving Tips from Norman Vincent Peale

- Sit relaxed in a chair with both feet lightly on the floor. Think of your mind as the surface of a storm-tossed lake. Now picture the waves subsiding, the water becoming as smooth as glass.

- Spend a few minutes reliving the most peaceful scenes you've ever beheld—a beach at sunset, a green valley in the hush of morning. They have a way of cleansing your mind of worries.

- Repeat—slowly, bringing out the melody in each—a series of calming words. "Peace, tranquility, serenity, quietness ..."

- Sit comfortably. Close your eyes and relax your muscles. Breathe naturally and repeat a word, phrase, or prayer (like "peace," "The Lord is my shepherd," or "shalom") silently or aloud. When other thoughts come to mind, let them go and return to your repetition. Do this for 10 minutes or so.

Don't you feel more relaxed? I know I do.

As you might know, my mom, Carol, and my grandma, Maxine, are huge inspirations to me in my life. My mom is one of the most positive people I have ever met. She always seems to have a smile on her face and a warm thing to say about everyone. Everyone loves her, and I have never heard a negative thing said about her by someone else. She goes about her life trying to help others and has fun doing it. So, where did she get that philosophy? It was her mother, Maxine. Maxine (my grandmother) lived by an optimist creed. She, too, was an amazing woman. Spending her life in the service of others. Always positive and forward-looking. Her belief in God and the creed is what guided her life. Here's that creed:

Promise Yourself

To be so strong that nothing can disturb your peace of mind.

To talk about health, happiness, and prosperity to every person you meet.

To make all your friends feel that there is something worthwhile in them.

To look at the sunny side of everything and make your optimism come true.

To think only of the best, to work only for the best, and to expect only the best.

To be just as enthusiastic about the success of others as you are about your own.

To forget the mistakes of the past and press on to the greater achievements of the future.

To wear a cheerful expression at all times and give a smile to every living creature you meet.

To give so much time to improving yourself that you have no time to criticize others.

To be too large for worry, too noble for anger, too strong for fear, and too happy to permit the presence of trouble.

To think well of yourself and to proclaim this fact to the world, not in loud words, but in great deeds.

To live in the faith that the whole world is on your side, so long as you are true to the best that is in you.

The Optimist Creed was authored in 1912 by Christian D. Larson, appearing in his book, Your Forces and How to Use Them.

"The only sure way for your people to lose is if they give up. Your lack of encouragement should never be the reason a person quits. A leader must always keep believing in people, no matter what."

Art Williams

One Recruit Away from an Explosion

It only takes ONE PERSON to believe in you, your vision, and your capabilities and draw it out of you to be successful. It takes one kind gesture, one motivating comment. You never know who you are influencing, or who you are talking to, who has the potential to become great. Every person I meet, whether working at KFC, McDonald's, or he's a corporate lawyer, I treat them all the same. I tell them they have the capability of becoming great or even more extraordinary. I get to know them; I get to know their family.

I have prospected and entertained thousands of people. I felt like I was just one recruit away from an explosion. I was just one person away from believing in me and seeing my vision that it drove me to get up every single day and try to push people to the next level. I wanted to help them master their craft and become a better version of themselves.

Every Saturday morning for twenty years, I trained people, and then after the training, I would go to lunch with them. I would spend time asking about their family, lives, goals, and dreams. I was investing in another human being. Trying to find out what the hot buttons were. What do they really want out of life? Do they have big goals and dreams? What were the desires that they wanted to achieve? Did they want their kids to go to college one day? Did they want that amazing dream car? What about the dream house on the beach? Beautiful mountain estate?

Every time a new recruit wanted to quit on me, I was able to take them back to that previous vision and get them to see that if they quit, what would they do? If they go back to their job, will their job give them that dream life? Because I understood why people wanted what they wanted, I could get them to hold on just a little bit longer. I'd get them to stick around to give their efforts time to compound. Believing in people is and always will be the most rewarding and best decision of my life.

"Always Build Personal Relationships...Get to know your people. Get to know their kids. Get to know their families.

Build meaningful lasting relationships. Don't be afraid to tell people you love them. Let them know you really care."

Art Williams

Six Foot Trophies

I believe in recognition. I believe in praise. That's why we are always giving out recognition. Shirts. Hats. Six-foot Trophies. Plaques. Dinners. Movies. Cash! Each and every month, we give out tributes for the prior month. We are trying to spot the next shining stars. Those breakout recruits who seem to be extra focused and determined to make their dreams come true. The recognition is just a way to let them know of their accomplishments. It's our way of saying, 'We appreciate you. You are special.'

It all has to do with human nature. You see, we all have basic needs. One of those needs is a feeling of accomplishment. We all have a flashing sign on our back that reads… Say something good to me. Make me feel important. Next time you get the opportunity to tell someone, 'Great job, you inspire me,' don't be shy. Say it!

Connection & Love

Did you know we all need to feel bonded with a cause? Why do people join clubs? Unions? Why do people volunteer for free? It's because the human spirit feels compelled to connect. They want to feel loved and to give love. Go ahead, tell that teammate you love them. Tell them, 'I appreciate you so much.' Again, when you don't do this, it's because your nasty EGO is getting in the way. Be vulnerable. Be open and be kind. Who knows, that kind word you give someone today could be the word that changes their lives forever.

Boss vs. Leader

As you now know, the best way to scale any business is by lifting people up. It's a boss vs. leader mentality. A boss makes you feel weak or inferior. A leader inspires you to become a better version of yourself. Realize that not everyone is built like you and operates differently. Here are a few differences between a boss and a leader:

- A boss has his own interests, and a leader puts his people first.
- A boss tells, and a leader leads.
- A boss demands respect; a leader earns it.
- A boss is dispensable in a company; a leader is indispensable:
- A boss instills fear, but the leader generates a great deal of excitement.
- A boss is not approachable, versus a leader always having her door wide open.
- A boss speaks in terms of 'I, me and myself but a leader always says 'We, our and us.'
- A boss encourages you to shut up and listen, but a leader encourages you to express who you are.
- A boss takes all the credit, and a leader gives lavish praise.

- A boss makes you feel as though you are lucky to just have a job, but a leader understands that without great people, they are nothing.

Being a leader is not easy, but it will be one of the most rewarding things you will ever do. To have the responsibility of helping people and changing lives. What's better than that? Now get out there and prospect, make new friends, build great new relationships and close, close, close.

The future is yours!

LAW 8 | MASTERING THE SALES GAME

MASTERING THE SALES GAME

"I am not judged by the number of times I fail, but by the number of times I succeed and the number of times I succeed is in direct proportion to the number of times I can fail and keep trying."

Tom Hopkins

Becoming A Prospecting Master

Prospecting is essential. If you don't make prospecting a way of life, I'm talking about meeting new people and building new relationships; creating a successful business will not be possible. I always tell teammates my title is 'Professional Friend Maker.' I make friends for a living because friends ultimately become recruits and clients or refer business. I'm not saying you make a friend for the sole purpose of selling them something or making an economic benefit. I'm saying my life is great because I spend a lot of my life meeting people and building relationships.

I always open doors for others. I smile at random people. I also do it to keep me in the habit of always being a nice person. It's not a fake thing--it's real. It just so happens that the benefit of that is people want to do business with me. They like me and trust me and feel my genuine care for them. Because this ultimately is a type of energy and frequency. You have to constantly be positive. I believe a life of prospecting and making new friends keeps me happier than most.

Remember, you have a duty as a human being to be happy. When you are happy, the world is happier. You bring joy and love to people, which is emitted in frequency.

Prospect as a Way of Life

Let's say I prospect a cashier at the grocery store. I smile at them, and they smile back, and I ask them how long they've been working there and tell them they seem like they're good with people and have they ever considered a career change if the money was right? It's that simple. You need to prospect for new recruits because recruits ultimately become the best clients. Plus, you will get better results when you offer an opportunity first versus trying to hawk your product.

I have systems on how to prospect for different scenarios: group presentations, churches, businesses, schools, police, and fire departments. For example, let's say you want to get a group presentation at a high school. First, get referred to and build a relationship with the decision-maker. Maybe that's the principal. Get them to see how your information can really make a difference in the lives of their teachers. You might use this angle… "My job is to come in and educate teachers on how money works." Convey how it can benefit their employees. And best of all, it's free to the organization. In my finance business, if an employee is more financially educated, they are less stressed. If they are less stressed, they're more productive and happier at work. Make it easy for the boss to see your value.

"A large social-media presence is important because it's one of the last ways to conduct cost-effective marketing. Everything else involves buying eyeballs and ears. Social media enables a small business to earn eyeballs and ears."

Guy Kawasaki

The World of Social Media

So how do you prospect on social media? The first step is to build your brand. So that means that you're gonna have to post daily. People have often said I don't like social media because I'm wasting lots of time looking at pictures of what people eat! I want to say, don't be a consumer of social media; instead, be a creator of social media. What that means is every day, you get up to add value to the world by posting content.

What kind of content do you ask? Pictures, videos, thoughts, tweets, reels, etc. So, what's the magic number? On Instagram, 3 to 5 posts per day and 20 stories per day. I think it's vital that you become relevant to your audience. Your goal should always be to not try and sell people about your product or your company every day. It's genuinely about giving away your content for free. But wait a minute, why would I give all my content away for free? Because if your content is worthy and valuable, people will consume it.

As they consume your content in their minds, you become the expert in your field. As you become the expert in your field, when that person consuming your content needs your product or service or even your opportunity, who will they think about? They think about you! Every company does it. Pepsi does it. Coke does it.

Disney does it. Starbucks does it. Every major corporation wants to get more eyeballs to see its logo. Their brand. Whenever you think about an apple, what do you think about? The Apple corporation. iPad and iPhones. When you see a mouse with big ears, the first thing that comes to your mind is Disneyland. So, if they do it, why wouldn't you want the world to see your logo? Why wouldn't you want the world to consume your face, voice, and thoughts every day?

By the way, prospecting through social media is a better, more efficient way of doing business. That's because when somebody contacts you through social media, they have probably been following you for quite some time. And because they've been following you, they're already half sold by the time you talk to them.

I love when new recruits contact me and ask me for information about my opportunity. Because I have a friendly social media presence, they trust me. One of the biggest challenges I see for young entrepreneurs is that they have a horrible social media presence. If you're in the financial world, why the heck are you posting pictures of your dog every day. Now I think your dog is nice, and you're proud of your dog, and you love your dog, but you're not selling dogs. You're selling financial services. So, every day, you should talk about financial services, talk about how I can make more money, give me value, teach me things and make me see you as an expert, not just some hack on the Internet.

The other takeaway is that your job is NOT to sell me every day. Stop telling me to buy your product. People hate commercials.

So why would you post commercials all day, every day? Give genuine value.

Give entertainment. Give inspiration. We've all heard it before... Build it, and they will come.

But I'm not Computer Savvy

I hear this all the time from entrepreneurs that have been in business for quite some time. They just like doing it the old-fashioned way. I'm not saying the old-fashioned way doesn't work; I'm just saying there's a better mousetrap. What better way is to create a large following on your social media to create the necessary leads to keep you busy bringing in business more often. I get it that you're not computer savvy. But you know what? You don't need to be.

Today, there are people who will do it for you. You just gotta get out of your own way and delegate. There's an app called Fiverr. This app is a marketplace full of hungry, motivated people that will do small jobs for you. Such as building your online presence. Creating content for you. Creating funnels and online lead generation systems. There's no excuse for getting left behind in today's virtual world.

"Find a product you believe in.

Those who are convinced are convincing."

Frank Beltran

Are You Afraid of Sales?

Create a BIG Picture Sales Culture. Get people unafraid of sales. A lot of people are afraid, so you have to talk about sales and explain how sales are a good thing. The most successful people can sell. They sell something, even people that aren't salespeople. Take a doctor, for example. They are selling you on why to take medicine to get better or getting an operation to save your life. A man sells a woman on marrying them forever. A musician plays with passion and sells his audience on his music. A teacher sells a kid on the importance of education.

Step number one, believe what you're selling is good and good for the world. We have paid over $151 million of death claims in my career. Our team has invested almost half of a billion dollars for the families we serve. My business pays millions per year in compensation to our agents. Think about how much difference we made in the lives of those people!

Understanding Your Market

Before I even go to an appointment to sell life insurance in my business, I need to make sure certain things are there for the market - married, with children, and they have a full-time job. If they don't have those things, I won't make the appointment. Why? Because they're not qualified and will be way less likely to buy. What about if a recruit comes into your business and doesn't have a market? Don't recruit them. Ouch! Well, you can recruit them but just don't spend a lot of time with them. Ouch again! Well, you can spend some time but just make it clear that if they don't go out and prospect to build a new market of contacts, they will not last in the business.

The number one mistake I made in business was spending too much time with the wrong people. People that were not coachable. People without a market or refusing to meet new people to try and grow their list of contacts. People that were not willing to create a real online brand. Ultimately, many of these people fell out of business simply because they refused to change. My job is to give people opportunities, but I can't win for them.

Calendly.com

Here's a neat tip… I use Calendly.com to allow my new recruits to book appointments in my calendar. This is so I don't have to go back and forth trying to find times to set appointments.

The best advantage with Calendly is it enables you to set schedules for all sorts of event types. You can allocate available times, blackout dates, automatically add buffer time, limit the number of events to the calendar within a day, and much more.

I send my new recruit a Calendly link, and they fill in the questions to make certain the appointment is, in fact, qualified. Next, Calendly automatically sends the booked appointment to my calendar with information for my review. Then Calendly works with Zoom to seamlessly create a Zoom link and emails to my newbie. The new recruit forwards that link to the prospect. Simple.

Step 1: Get Calendly.

Step 2: Set up your Calendar questions.

Step 3: Set your calendar. Block out times you can't book appointments. For example, your kid's soccer game or your date night.

Step 4: Make a shortcut for the link in your phone.

The point is to qualify all appointments to maximize your results. Unqualified appointments take you away from productive opportunities to make more sales and recruits!

"Service is a given, what separates me is, I bring value."

Marty Rodriguez

The BEST Referral System

The best referral process is the recruit and train model. If I recruit you, I will train you in your warm market. It is the most genius system in the world. If you take me to see your best friend, chances are we will do business. Did you know, most people have 1000 contacts on their phone? Why would anyone ever say, I don't know anyone. Everyone has someone to see. And check this out, if I close one sale and get ten referrals, that gives me ten more opportunities to sell and recruit. If I close five out of those ten referrals and then get ten referrals from those five sales, that's another fifty prospects to go see! Not to mention, what if I recruit ten people and they have a list of twenty-five people in their close contacts? That's another 250 prospects! I built my business from this system.

Always ask people, who do you know? Who do you know that has young kids? Why young kids? Well, in my business, we sell life insurance. When someone has young kids, there is a high likelihood that the prospect will want to purchase a policy to protect those kids. Every business will be different. You might sell cars. What's your market? Everyone over sixteen or legal driving age, right? You can ask for referrals through group presentations from what we call silent partners who provide referrals for us.

The cool thing is that the silent partner can get paid for giving referrals! There's also a beneficiary close system in my business. If the husband and wife die together, the money is given to someone over eighteen who is responsible for children. They give me a name and set up an appointment to explain the process, and I can sell to them to become a client.

Setting Appointments

We've talked a lot about setting appointments, and that's because it's the first thing to get your foot in the door. The easiest way to create a referral is by teaching someone to set an appointment with someone else for them to recruit. I have an 'exciting, training, opinion, help me' script. I call you up and say, "I'm excited, I'm going through training, and I want your opinion. Would you help me?" This is a warm market lead. If the recruit has credibility, the prospect will say yes 99% of the time. Then, you give them two days and times (alternate of choice) and have them pick. When they pick, the appointment is booked! Another way to book a warm market prospect for a time is to text them.

Here's what I text:

Hi John, I NEED YOUR HELP! I'm in a program to get certified and licensed as a financial representative, and I need to complete twenty hours of training through Zoom. As a favor to me, will you take twenty minutes to help me? I'm not sure whether you're interested or not. I included my manager in this text. Thanks!

Three reasons this works so well. Number one, it's a text. 90%+ texts are opened. Number two, the prospect will book a time because the manager is in the text group. They usually set a time out of fear of making the new recruit look bad. And number three, if the prospect asks a question they can't answer, the manager can jump in and answer it. Or better yet, make the call and book the appointment through voice. Plus, if a new recruit says they are working hard but not trying to book appointments, you will know this simply because they did not include you in any text messages.

Stamp this in your brain!! Without appointments, you will not sell or recruit. You will not make money. You won't build a team. You will never be rich. You will never create massive passive residual income! The moral of the story? Spend most of your time creating new appointments.

I would make sure I spent at least three hours straight booking my week every Sunday night. I would lock myself in my office or in my car and relentlessly book my own personal sales calls or inspire my new recruits to get their training appointments booked for that week. I did this consistently for ten years! By the way, I always had my new recruits book their appointments because I wanted them to be self-sufficient. Also, if they knew how to do it, they would be able to teach their teams later on.

Daymond John, the founder of FUBU and star of Shark Tank, says, "It's okay to rely on the people around you for help, your mentors, friends, or family. If you can't sell the people closest to you on your ideas or product, who can you convince to buy your product? Close connections can help you network and provide moral support if you're struggling."

When he was a struggling twenty-something, Daymond asked his mom for help. She even took out a second mortgage to help him get his business off the ground! It's okay to ask for help. It's okay to lean on others as you work your way up the ladder of success. You know the Universe rewards the bold, right? So, what are you waiting for? Be brave. ASK someone for help today!

Are you TYING people down?

Did you know that professional salespeople know things most rookies don't know? Here are some simple but effective ways to become more influential with your words.

1. What is a tie-down question?

A question at the end of a sentence that demands a "yes."

- Joe and Mary, protecting your family's financial future makes sense to you, doesn't it?

- You're excited about having a solid financial plan, aren't you?

2. What is an inverted Tie-Down?

Putting the tie-down on the front for a warmer feeling.

- John, Mary, aren't you excited about having a solid financial plan?

- John and Mary, isn't it true that your family could be financially devastated if you pass away tomorrow?

- John, Mary, doesn't it make sense to you to protect your family's financial future?

3. What is the Alternate of Choice?

A question with two answers. Either answer is a minor agreement leading toward the final decision. Best used for an appointment time, location, type of investment, and closing on the final money amount.

- I have Thursday or Friday evening open this week. Which night would be better for you?

- If you had a choice between this one and this one, which one would you feel would be in your family's best interest for the long run?

4. What is the Porcupine?

Answering the correct question with a question to get the client to elaborate or open up.

- Client: Does this plan also cover the kids?

- You: If the plan did include the kids, would you feel that this is the plan for you?

The best closers I know are always asking. They are curious. They genuinely want to give the prospect what they want. If I ask good questions and get reliable information from a prospect, I can then guide them to deciding in their best interest.

"If you let your emotions get high, your bargaining power will be low. Make sure you don't negotiate from a position of need when making a deal."

Sharon Lechter

The Closing Process

Wanna get more people to say YES? I believe a lot of little yeses creates a big yes at the end. Closing is not hard when you know how to ask questions. When you ask the appropriate questions at the appropriate time, people more often than not tell you 'Yes.' Closing is always about questions. I might ask someone if you were to, God forbid, pass away, would you want a lower, same, or higher standard of living? When they say at least the same, even subconsciously, they're saying yes. They're selling themselves.

I ask people questions to come to a conclusion to see for themselves that they need what I am selling. And I also get them to see that others are buying because most people want to do what others do. I get them to say ten little yeses before getting the big yes. And I mostly get yeses because my questions are direct and straightforward.

When you develop genuine trust and then ask the right questions, closing is fun, easy, and so profitable!

LAW 9 |REPLICATING THE PROCESS

"Leaders are focused on using their vision and courage to do great things. This means challenging the way things are done and then sharing the journey with others."

Lewis Howes

To build a strong foundation of recurring income, there is one thing you need to solidify. And that is a strong replicated army of YOU. Once you have mastered your skills, knowledge, niche, and service offerings, you must learn to master systems and processes. When you master systems and processes - this will be the true key to your freedom.

You see, people who are masters at their craft are the true masters of building wealth. But to truly become free and not require yourself to work day and night to the bone, you must learn to relinquish control. You must shed your ego to the point that you are willing to teach others your craft and recruit intelligent people who have the skillset and knowledge to build your business. That is when you can replicate the process. When you master your craft and start making a solid income stream, you will naturally and organically have people follow you. They will be drawn to your business acumen and skill mastery and want to know what you did and how.

Do not be deterred in this.

I myself am a walking testimony to the power of replication. I knew at an early age that although I loved the process of making money and going in for the close, I did not want to do this day in and day out for the rest of my life! I didn't want to be that guy strolling around with my briefcase at seventy trying to close deals. Most people keep their ideas and knowledge to themselves because they are scared of others replicating them - not knowing this is the true key to lasting freedom. When you are sought to be copied, you know you are indeed onto something BIG.

The only way to build a business that will create passive income is to clone different versions of you and direct them or create streamlined, automated processes, so you don't need to be present and operating. If you think about it logically, every big business and corporation has created systems and processes to duplicate successful outcomes. Amazon. Disney. Walmart. Target. Home Depot. Tesla. Apple. JP Morgan. Airbnb. Uber. They all do it, and so should you.

Create the Vision

Your team needs to feel that they can create passive income by following the same path as you. This is where it gets fun and also meaningful. This is where you build purpose. When people buy into your vision, they are now inclined to be influenced by your mission, values, and something more significant than the ego and, ironically, more than money. As paradoxical as this sounds, when you create a vision and higher purpose, the money will just come. This is how you build an army of motivated followers and a contingent 'volunteer workforce.' Remember, people will always work much harder for something bigger than just for you. They must know that their hustle and grind is for their family's future, for something larger than life, for the benefit of society, not just yours.

"People don't want a "boss. They want a leader."

Daniel Alonzo

A business partner enables them to achieve their goals and, ultimately, some level of financial success, recognition for their contributions, and total freedom. This is universal law and fundamental human desire.

Sell The Dream

Now that you know this, you have to sell the dream. Show your team and the people around you a lifestyle that is possible. Find out what motivates them, what are the fundamental basic human needs? We are all driven by our desire for basic needs, growth, comfort, love, belonging, recognition, and eventually, self-actualization. On a psychological level, we are all driven by the need to truly elevate ourselves, our lives and reach our true potential.

Maslow's Hierarchy of Needs

What will look like when they win? We call it painting the picture. Paint a portrait of where they will live, what their bank account will look like, where they will travel, how many lives they will impact for good, and most importantly, all the FREEDOM they will get by following your plan. Selling the dream is about getting people to see farther than they can see by themselves. Stretching their thoughts.

You see, when you are an employee, and then you get thrown into trying to build a business, you see things from an employee mentality. When someone says, you can live in that house on the hill, you tend to doubt it because you don't know anyone that's an employee living in a multi-million-dollar home behind a guarded gate with freedom. You only believe what you know.

When I was first introduced to entrepreneurship, I made $7 per hour. I was broke. I was driving a Nissan pickup truck with no air conditioning, still living with my parents. The guy that sold me the dream said, 'you can make $100K per year! You will one day drive the best and fastest cars in the world.' He said I would live in a mansion. He continued, 'you will one day travel to some of the best resorts.' And lastly, he said, 'you will accumulate millions and millions of dollars, so you will have freedom, choices, and options to do what you want, when you want, with who you like.' Oh, and then he said one more thing . . . 'You will have all of this before you're thirty.' My eyes lit up. My brain went into overdrive. I started to believe. I got focused. I got to work. I followed his process. And the rest is history. Now, that's how you sell the dream!

"I want to take my success and replicate it with other artists."

Jake Paul

Replicate Results by Training and Testing Your Team

You need to become results-oriented, period. Many people go into sales and are not results-oriented, and they don't see progress. Someone new on my team will call me at night and talk about how they went on a great appointment where everyone was excited, and

I'll ask what they closed. And they'll say, 'I spent three hours with the prospect but didn't close' . . . and then go into all the reasons why.

They wanted to give more information. They wanted to build the relationship stronger. I would ask, 'did you give quotes? Did you try to close?' They would say, 'well, I'm going back next week to ask for the business.' They weren't focused on results. They weren't focused on making money or building a team. Remember, if you don't get results, you don't make money. If you don't make money, you don't inspire anyone. If you don't encourage anyone, you don't build leaders. And if you don't have leaders, there's no big business. If there's no big business, there's no passive income.

Results matter. The people will stop following you. I close on the first night because if I do, my new recruit gets excited. If they get excited, they want that feeling of excitement of success and want it repeatedly, and if they get it, you both will have success. You always want to inspire because that will bring you long-term results. Plus, if you don't make money, you will go out of business. When you inspire, more people want to follow you, and then the bigger the team gets - the bigger the team, the more freedom.

TRAIN, TRAIN, TRAIN

You need to have consistent training for your team. Yes, we talked about the initial training, but I mean making sure training is constant and consistent. For 20+ years, I went to Saturday morning training sessions to teach and train my team. I showed up and was consistent. Even though I had systems in place where they could learn independently, I believe it's crucial to often train in person or on

Zoom. This is how you can connect on a deeper level with your people. They see your passion and love for what you do.

When I was sixteen, I worked in the parade department at Disneyland as a float driver. When I first got started, Disney put you through an indoctrination program. Eight hours a day for a week! Watching videos and training so we could be immersed in Disney culture. It was brainwashing. How to speak. How to dress. How to greet guests. New words. New ways of thinking. That's what I do.

Your team must feel great about your company and what you stand for. Motivation is good, but you have to be a hardcore trainer. I see many leaders who don't train and are just trying to motivate. I roleplay my presentation, which seems boring, but the boring things make you rich. I tell them to throw objections at me, and I overcome them. I test them in every scenario to be sure they are getting it. You need to test your teams when they're ready. Test, test, test to verify their confidence.

I have a question for you, if you consider yourself good at your business, what would happen if you had one hundred people as good as you? Would you be more or less successful?

How to Replicate the Process

You get what you expect. You see, I believe that what separates me from most was that I believed that what would bring me lasting freedom was the duplicating of me. Seriously, I wanted a business that wouldn't really need me to be successful. I wanted to ensure that I wouldn't have to worry about money coming in if I was traveling the world.

I know what you're thinking; that's not possible. Well, the truth is, you do have to grind in the beginning. In the beginning, you must put in the time, work hard and build your foundation. But the ultimate goal is to have multiple locations and leaders that want what you want. They are trying to build a business like yours. Because they are in the grinding stage, you can now live free. That's why replicating or duplicating you is so important!

1999

In 1999 I became a Regional VP of the company. I had gotten a lot of results and was making a decent amount of money. I was #1 in the country! So, I moved up. This was a promotion that allowed me to expand and build multiple locations. The first thing I did was record my first-night presentation. I went to a guy that duplicated tapes, and I paid him a lot of money to make me hundreds of tapes! I distributed these audio cassettes to my team and told them to learn my words.

Learn my system. I also wrote a manual for people that liked to read. I literally listened to my recorded words and typed them into the computer. I then got my little brother Jeff (he's actually way taller than me, lol) to make hundreds of copies of the manual. My brother is a major key to why we replicated and grew the business so fast. Jeff even built a website so people could watch online and buy CDs and manuals independently. All the while, I was recruiting and selling personally. I would do this busy work early in the morning or late at night. This is what people miss. They get so involved in trying to build a system but don't actually produce and get individual results.

The results are important because it proves that your system actually works. That's why my team wanted to learn the material. Because they saw me making money and having success. I told them that if they could get good enough at the business, they could also become a regional vice president and build a business like mine. My team got excited. Within my first few years as a VP, we had opened up six new locations! Today, due to technology, we have so many cool ways to replicate ourselves:

- **Apps**
- **YouTube videos**
- **Websites**
- **Zoom**
- **One on one Training videos**
- **Group training videos**
- **Manuals**
- **Books**

Decide today that you will use technology to build systems and processes so you can duplicate yourself. Your future freedom is counting on it!

Tell Your People How YOU Did It

I was constantly explaining to people how I did it. I would call all my key people to share my results. I was so specific about what I did and how I did it. What objections did I get? How did I overcome that objection? How did I meet the prospect? What did I say to actually get the appointment? When the prospect tried to cancel the appointment, how did I get in the door anyways? If the prospect was being unruly, how did I take control of the conversation and then close?

The chatting that happened late at night with my key players was so important. I was slowly embedding in their minds the culture of winning. A culture of results. The culture of training and duplicating. Because they read my books and listened to my videos, they would get their people to do the same. That's the power of replication!

A Whole NEW World

Do you believe it! We are now in the decade of the 2020s. Technology is shaping our lives. Did you know that if you are in your fifties and don't smoke, you are almost certain to live to over 100? The scientists are actually making spray-on skin. They can make an ear with a 3D printer. You will either embrace this new world or get left behind.

I get it. It's hard. So, fucking what. Do it anyway. You are going to have to learn how new apps work.

You don't like social media? Well, if you want to get others inspired by you, you will have to build a brand. Get some more eyeballs on you now. If you are in sales, start with selling yourself. Then sell the world your story. Sell the world how what you do can help them. Your product and service must be something you believe in. And by the way, if you are on a limited budget, you will have to figure a lot of this tech shit out on your own.

That doesn't mean you will have to master technology and become a computer nerd genius; you will just have to learn the basics. Then as time goes by and you become more financially secure, delegate the stuff you don't want to do to others. I don't edit my YouTube anymore. My son Max does. He's a stud. I did in the beginning. I do very little tedious paperwork. My assistant helps with that. I don't pay bills. My Mom comes to my house each week and makes sure my bills are paid, taxes are paid, and my Quicken is updated and organized. I don't clean my own home or wash my own clothes. My housekeeper, Patti of twenty years, does that. But I did in the beginning. I did so many things at the outset that I no longer do today. Always be reminded that you can't make excuses and be successful simultaneously. Winners always find a way!

Different Types of Scaling and Replicating the Process

Multi-level marketing is a business structure or practice in which an individual seller earns commissions from direct sales and from the sales of the seller's recruits, those recruited by the seller's recruits, and so on. Who should consider this type of business marketing? Anyone that wants to make more money, either full or part-time.

When I was twenty-one, and my best friend recruited me into the multi-level marketing business, I was very skeptical. I said, 'isn't this like a Pyramid scheme? Do I have to recruit all my family and friends?' He said, no, it's a business like any other. He went on to say it was like the real estate business. There's a broker, and there is an agent. When the agent makes a sale, because the broker maintains the office and trains the agent, they receive a cut of the commissions.

Therefore, the broker has a vested interest in helping the agent make as much money as possible.

The slight difference with multi-level is that you can recruit as many people as possible, and most people begin their careers on a part-time basis. So, therefore, the upside potential is endless. And of course, if you can recruit and train lots of motivated people into your organization, that is how you create massive passive cash flow.

Network marketing, unfortunately, has had some well-deserved reputation issues. Mainly because there are unlimited amounts of recruiting that's involved. When you have a situation like that, you will attract many unscrupulous people. Also, if the recruiter is not a good trainer, the new recruit might make lots of mistakes along the way, furthering the damage to the company's reputation. Today, most publicly traded multi-level marketing companies are held to rigorous standards. Looking for a company that adheres to compliance excellence is a good place to start.

So even knowing my initial experience and understanding of this type of business was not a good one, I found that multi-level marketing is one of the best, least expensive, most profitable ways to get really rich.

Franchising Opportunities are the right or license granted to an individual or group to market a company's goods or services in a particular territory. We all know the story of the most famous franchise, McDonald's!

The McDonald Brothers

Dick and Mac McDonald started McDonald's in California after moving there to seek opportunities. They didn't feel like New England was gonna give them a chance to make their fortune. Initially starting in and failing in the movie business, they proved the concept of the drive-in restaurant. In 1948 they introduced their speedy service system featuring $.15 hamburgers. That success led them to further explore the franchising concept. The brothers recruited owners to pay them $950 and sold fourteen franchises!

Enter Ray Kroc - He was from Chicago and left high school in the 10th grade to fight in World War I Red Cross Ambulance Corps. Luckily the war ended before he was sent overseas. In 1939 he started to work as a distributor for the Multimixer (a milkshake mixing machine) company. Eventually, he made it to the McDonald's brothers in 1954, saw their vision, and signed on as a franchise agent. In 1955, he opened the first McDonald's east of the Mississippi river! Ray's original focus was to recruit and offer his opportunity to 1000 people in America!

He probably could never imagine that McDonald's continues to grow worldwide. In 1967 they even opened up in Canada in Puerto Rico. As of this writing, the company has over 39,198 restaurants in over 100 countries. That's a lot of recruits! You might be asking, why do you keep referring to the restaurant owners as recruits? That's because each and every one of those restaurants has owners that paid between $750,000-2.5 million to buy a franchise. They got recruited into a vision that if they build the business, they can generate passive income from each location that they own. They get money and time freedom if they recruit and train people to run those locations! I mean, think about it, they get paid a small percentage on every hamburger sale. Every French fries' order. Even every milkshake!

So, the point here is mass distribution can create massive passive income. Don't ever get caught up in what **UN**successful people say and believe. Most unsuccessful people have jobs. One source of income, distribution, is a foreign word to them.

Stamp this in your brain . . . Every business thinks about recruiting people and growing their distribution. Every sports organization dream of recruiting more great people. Every church prays that they attract great people to expand the Word. Whether you are a real estate broker, financial services broker, multi-level business leader, pastor, or coach, your job is to recruit, train, and develop new leaders that will ultimately increase your organizational success!

LAW OF NATURE - PARETO PRINCIPLE

The Pareto principle is also known as the 80/20 rule. It's named after economist Vilfredo Pareto, and it basically says that 80% of the consequences come from 20% of the causes. Asserting that there's an unequal relationship between outputs and inputs. It's not balanced. So, if you're in business, be reminded that 80% of your production will come from 20% of the top performers.

Here's an example of the Pareto principle. Let's just say you own your own financial services company, and you want to use the principal to help you manage your clients. Remember that not every client provides the same income to the advisor. Therefore, if an advisory practice has 100 clients, 80% of the advisor's revenue will come from the top 20 clients. These clients have the highest assets and create the most commissions. Spend more time with those clients. Send more gifts. Send more cards. Follow up more often. What about if you're a recruiter and trying to build a business of top salespeople? The idea here tells us to focus 80% of our time building and training the top 20%.

One of the biggest mistakes I made in business throughout the years was spending too much time with the wrong people. I often spent time with people trying to convince them to create a great life for their families by working hard and staying focused. More often than not, those people let me down. They lied. They flaked. They disappointed me. They wasted my time. But in truth, if I had followed the 80/20 rule, I would've spent less time with the time wasters and MORE time with the people that showed high motivation and strong desire.

To sum things up, as a new entrepreneur, your job is to recruit, sell, lead, build, organize, etc. Yes, those things are important, sure. Just don't forget to replicate. Duplicate. This is how you will get your

Wealth on the Beach! So, you got your Wealth on the Beach? Awesome!

Now, let's talk about getting really wealthy and keeping that Wealth...

LAW 10 | MASTERING FINANCIAL INTELLIGENCE

Build an Actual Plan

"There is nothing wrong in wanting to get rich. The desire for riches is really the desire for a richer, fuller, and more abundant life, and that desire is praiseworthy."

Wallace D. Wattles

O ne of the most important aspects of becoming financially free and truly wealthy is to develop and master financial literacy and intelligence. Yet an overwhelming amount of the world's population floats with little to no plan of how to build their wealth and manage their finances.

Seems alarming? Yes. Unfortunately, the reality we live in? Yes.

Why do you think that majority of the world's finances and capitalist structures and businesses are managed by the top 1%?

To truly become financially free and achieve the life of your dreams, there is one central thing you must do. Get your head around mastering financial intelligence and developing yourself a system and managing your finances to truly grow.

Do you have a PERSONALIZED STRATEGY FOR FINANCIAL SECURITY?

A financial needs analysis is how I figured out my goals to become financially free.

If, like many people, you're in the dark about your finances. You pay your bills each month and do your best to prepare for the future. But the truth is, there's only so much money to go around, and preparing for the future can be overwhelming.

One of the essential building blocks in establishing a firm financial foundation is determining the difference between 'wants' and 'needs.' Sounds simple, doesn't it? A 'want' is something you don't require for basic survival, and a 'need' is something you just have to live. Yet sometimes it can be hard to tell where a 'want' begins and a 'need' ends -especially where the immediate family is concerned.

Think about it, every business in the world plans for their finances. They do a profit and loss daily. They monitor their inventory. They have regular meetings to discuss finances. These companies even cut expenses if they feel their profit is too low. Financial health is all about the choices you make over the long term. I always taught my clients to build their plans like you build a home. Start with the foundation, and then work your way up!

Good Debt Vs. Bad Debt

Bad Debt is a disease. The reason that so many people do not invest early is because of BAD DEBT. You know what that is. It's credit cards at 24.99% compounding daily. It's that $700 television you bought on a credit card that, in the end, will cost you $2,500! Once and for all, it's time for you to break the cycle.

Let's start STACKING. Here's how it works.

By considering the interest rate and amount of debt, debt stacking identifies a way for you to pay off your debts. You begin

125

by making consistent payments on all of your debts. The debt that debt stacking suggests you pay off first is called your target account. When you pay off the target account, you roll the amount you were paying toward your following target account. As each debt is paid off, you continue this process. Debt stacking allows you to make the same total monthly payment toward all of your debt and works best when you do not accrue any new debts.

You continue this process until you have paid off all of your debts. When you finish paying off your debts, you can apply the amount you were paying towards your debt toward creating wealth and financial independence!

The RULE of 72

Have you ever heard of the Rule of 72? Why is this rule so important to understand?

The 72 rule is a formula that calculates how long it will take for your money to double.

Some investment accounts provide higher interest yields than others. If you invest in low-interest investments, it could take hundreds of years to double your money, simply because the interest you receive is so low. For example, the federal average for standard savings accounts is just 0.04 percent as of 2021. If you perform the rule of 72 on this interest rate, it will take you 1,800 years just to double your money.

On the contrary, if a mutual fund or other investment pays you 12%, your money would double every six years! Now you understand why the banks and insurance companies love you. You give them your money, they invest it, make tons of interest, and they pay you next to nothing. Don't fall for the scam.

"Remember that the only purpose of money is to get you what you want, so think hard about what you value and put it above money."

Ray Dalio

High Cost of Waiting

How much interest have you earned on your savings in the past five years? The number one answer is less than 1%. On a $50,000 balance, that would turn into only $55,256 in ten years!

If that's you, don't be ashamed. Most people around the globe have very little to show after a lifetime of working 9-5 day after day, week after week, year after year. The main goal of this section is to express the significant importance of investing now.

According to Bankrate's recent Money Pulse survey, 54% of Americans are not investing at all. Among millennials ages 18 to 35, just 66% are not investing any amount. In all my years sitting with families guiding their financial futures, I always taught them the younger you start investing, the more you can reap the benefits of compounding and long-term market gains.

According to Liz Weston over at MSN Money –"Someone who puts $4,000 a year into retirement accounts starting at 22 can have $1 million by age 62, assuming 8% average annual returns. Wait ten years to start contributing, and you'd have to put in more than twice as much – $8,800 a year – to reach the same goal."

Conversely, the longer you say, 'not yet' and wait for 'someday,' the more you have to contribute later on just to catch up. The opportunity cost of not investing now is high and very real.

But I CAN'T AFFORD TO INVEST . . . In Bankrate's survey, 46% of millennials said lack of money was their reason for not investing in stocks.

Having spent a lot of time looking inside the financial lives of Millennials and Gen Zs, I know that not being able to 'afford to invest' is, in fact, a reality for many people. That said, it doesn't have to be. Do whatever it takes to get your finances in order to begin investing NOW.

Where is MY Money?

Financial software might be overkill if you just need a tool to track your spending. But using a financial app will surely make your life more organized. I would spend an hour per week making sure I knew where the money was. My credit cards would be linked to the software. It allowed me to stay organized financially. As money flowed in, I made sure to categorize all the spending so I could do two things . . .

#1 Never miss a legitimate write-off. Remember, taxes are your biggest expense. We will talk more about that later.

#2 The financial app allowed me to visually see how much money was in all accounts so I could move excess money into savings. I would grow savings to a healthy 25K-50K & then I would deploy that money into better ROI investments such as my stocks, mutual funds, real estate & tax-deductible accounts.

My plan was to leave my checking account with very little money. Out of sight, out of mind. That way, I would always be pressed to make more. Most people make money and then immediately try to spend it. Not me. I was focused on becoming financially free. I was trying to create streams of income. I wasn't trying to impress anyone with my stuff. At the end of the day, the stuff will fade and get old. When you are starting to make money, your job is to keep it so you can compound the money. Albert Einstein said that compound interest is one of the most powerful things in the world! Ultimately, one day soon, you will be able to live off the interest that your accounts and investments will produce. That way, whether you work or don't work, your lifestyle won't change. Staying organized financially was the key to me saving my first million by 28!

"If you don't have $1 million saved, you need to stop buying stupid shit!"

Daniel Alonzo

Thou Shall Budget

Why should you budget? Well, because you need to understand where all the money is going. I would review my budget many times throughout the year. I would add and remove things accordingly. Am I wasting money in some areas? Are there too many subscriptions just sucking my money away? Why am I spending so much on eating out? The grocery bill is ridiculously high. Could we cut that down?

During my first seven years working toward financial independence, I spent so little on groceries. I shared meals at restaurants. Shopped at clothing stores that offered name brands for less! Even when I was making 300K per year, I was driving a used 10K Nissan Maxima. I figured every dollar spent I could invest. At one point, I was investing 50% of my income! Sacrifice? Yes. In the end, was it worth it? 100%!!

Are you Checking Your Checking

I always treated my credit card like a checking account. Every time I spend money on my credit card, I come home that night and mentally deducted it from my checking account. At the end of the month, the money was in my account to pay off my credit card. Think about all the money I saved in interest and fees! Again, more money to deploy to other investments! I'm proud to say that I've never paid one dime in interest to credit cards in all my years in business. Those credit card companies sure hate me!

Never Use Cash

Let's talk cash. Have you ever met that guy that always keeps a wad of cash in his pocket? He's always tipping here and tipping there. Pays for the meal with cash. Paying for clothing with cash. Paying for groceries with cash. I was never that guy. Why? Because people tend to not write off cash on their taxes. Plus, we forget about items that we pay in cash. And we tend to not track cash. Just think about it this way, if I buy an item for $100 and my tax rate it's 30%, and I don't write it off, I lose $30! Every $30 counts. Doesn't it?

Nobody's going to care about your money like you care about money. Are you a small business entrusting all of your income, expenses, and taxes to someone without double-checking their work? I actually do all of my own accounting. My business is not an inventory business with minimal expenses, so it's pretty easy. But, if you get to a point where you need someone to track your spending and expenses, make sure you double-check their work. Don't get lazy in this area because it could cost you millions.

Billy 🎼

Ever heard of Billy Joel? After the Rockstar's 1979 separation, Billy went to his ex-wife's brother, Frank, and asked him to take over his finances. Can you believe it? Frank stole millions! But Billy had no reason not to trust him. They were so close that Frank was the godfather of Billy's daughter, Alexa. Billy was on the road a lot and didn't double-check Frank's work. This happens to so many small businesses. You get so busy making money you forget to take care of the money you already made! For me, I like to sit in front of my computer at least once per week to review the money. Review the investments. Review the plan.

People can build wealth and make a lot of money through their business, but it can be lost or stolen unless you have a healthy financial system for your business and personal income.

Creating Financially Successful Habits

Part of creating wealth also means getting smart about all of your finances. Stop all non-essential spending. You want to actually be financially successful, not trying to look like it. I bought a $400K home when I could have purchased a multi-million dollar one. You also need to have a foundation of financial education. And you need an attitude of becoming financially successful to go with it. There's also some basic budgeting and tracking I can teach you. You need to use all of this to create a routine of financial success.

Burn that Money 🔥

Did You know that taxes are your most significant expense? Let me ask you a question. Would you ever take your money, lay it on the floor, light a match, and burn that money? If your answer is no, then why don't you pay more attention to your taxes? I love my country just as much as you, but did you know that we have a constitutional duty to pay less in taxes legally? Why is the government spending $300 for a hammer? Because they didn't work for that $300. The money was just magically given to them.

You work hard for your money, don't you? Course you do. So why wouldn't you protect it? This is why you need to get organized and make sure that tax planning is a part of your overall plan. Here's a couple of tips on making better choices when it comes to taxes:

Taxes are one of the most critical issues facing small and growing businesses. Like a company's profits, its annual tax bill will reflect the owner's skills and knowledge. Business owners need to be sure that they are meeting all of their taxman responsibilities and seizing every opportunity to reduce their taxes. These tax tips will ensure Mr. Government is not getting more than his due.

Writing It Off: Deductions. Businesses can deduct all "ordinary and necessary" business expenses from their revenues to reduce taxable income. Some deductions are obvious expenditures in areas like business travel, equipment, salaries, or rent. But the rules governing write-offs aren't always straightforward. Don't overlook these potential deductions:

Business losses - To reduce taxes, business losses can be deducted against a business owner's personal income. If a business owner's losses exceed personal income for the year, some of the business losses can be used to reduce taxable income in future years. Trips that combine business and pleasure. If more than half of a business trip is devoted to business, deduct the traveling costs and other business-related expenses.

Employee Taxes - If a business has employees, various taxes will have to be withheld from their salaries. Among them: Withholding. Social Security (FICA), Medicare, and federal and state income taxes must be withheld from employees' pay. Employer matching. Businesses must match the FICA and Medicare taxes and pay them with employees. Unemployment tax. Companies must pay federal and state unemployment taxes.

Quarterly Estimated - This area trips up many entrepreneurs and is especially vexing for home-based businesses. Failure to keep up with estimated tax bills can create cash flow problems and the potential for punishing IRS penalties. Among the issues are: Who should pay? A business probably must pay quarterly estimated taxes if the total tax bill in a given year will exceed $500. How much should you pay? By the end of the year, 90 percent of the tax owed or 100 percent of last year's tax must be paid (the figure is 110 percent if a business's income exceeds $150,000). Businesses can subtract their expenses from their income each quarter and apply their income tax rate (and any self-employment tax rate) to the resulting figure (their quarterly profit).

Sales Taxes - Most services remain exempt from sales tax, but most products are taxable (typical exceptions are food and drugs). If a business owner sells a product or service subject to sales tax, they must register with the state's tax department. Then taxable and nontaxable sales must be tracked and included on the company's sales tax return. Having what is considered a 'presence' in a state is the criteria used by the IRS to determine whether or not you are liable for paying state sales tax. If you do not have a physical presence in another state but sell items via the Internet or by catalog in that state, you can be subject to a state's 'use tax,' but typically not to their state sales tax. A "presence" in another state does not necessarily mean that you have a retail outlet in that state. If you have an office, warehouse, or employees working for you in that state, the IRS may consider you to have a presence in that state. Make sure you know your sales tax responsibilities in all states in which you are doing business.

Keep Tax Documents for at Least Seven Years. Good record-keeping saves money. Some things like copies of business tax returns, licenses, incorporation papers, and capital equipment expenses should be preserved indefinitely. Keep any tax-related documents (e.g., expense receipts, client 1099 forms, and vehicle mileage logs) for seven years.

Charitable Contributions - Unless your business is a C corporation, charitable contributions typically "flow through" the business and are claimed as deductions on the individual tax returns of the shareholders of the company. That's true whether you're running a sole proprietorship, partnership, limited liability corporation, or S corporation.

If you want to get the maximum tax benefits, you should know these basic rules:

Contributions - Only contributions to charities listed as "qualified organizations" by the IRS are deductible. Consult IRS Publication 78 for a list of qualified organizations or search online at the IRS home page.

Contributions of more than $250 require a letter of receipt from the qualified organization. For contributions of less than $250, a canceled check is sufficient. In general, property donations can be deducted for their fair market value at the time of the contribution. You cannot deduct a contribution that has already been written off as a depreciated asset. You cannot deduct the value of time or services that you volunteer. You cannot deduct the part of a contribution that benefits you. If you receive a gift in exchange for a charitable donation, you can deduct only the amount of the contribution that exceeds the value of the gift. You can generally deduct contributions only in the year you make them. Pledged contributions cannot be deducted until they are actually paid.

Important Tax Deadlines for Businesses - April 15 isn't the only important tax date for business owners. The following dates are important to keep in mind: Annual returns. Most annual returns are due April 15 for unincorporated companies and S corporations. C corporations must file annual corporate returns within two-and-a-half months after the close of their fiscal year. Estimated taxes. Estimated taxes are due four times a year: April 15, June 15, September 15, and January 15. Pay your taxes quarterly to eliminate any penalties. Sales taxes. Sales taxes are due quarterly or monthly, depending on the rules in your state. Employee taxes.

Depending on the size of your payroll, employee taxes are due weekly, monthly or quarterly.

Deducting Loans - Most business loans are not considered business income. One notable exception is a situation in which you negotiate with a creditor or lender to reduce your debt. If any debt is forgiven, you will owe taxes on this amount. On the other hand, business loans can offer substantial tax benefits. The principal and interest you pay on your loan are business expenses, and you can deduct them from your taxes as such. To take advantage of a tax deduction, you must report the total amount of the loan, and the assets and expenditures financed must be necessary to operate the business.

Tax Audits - The very thought of an IRS audit is enough to make most business owners break into a cold sweat. But not all audits are created alike: There are several different types of tax audits, ranging from simple requests for a particular piece of information to comprehensive reviews that cover every aspect of a business.

Correspondence Audit - This is a relatively simple procedure in which the IRS asks you to document an item on your return by a specified date. This is usually a routine test for compliance with certain items on your return.

Office Audit - The IRS may ask you to report to a nearby IRS office and document one or more items on your return. You may be able to send them copies of this proof in advance of the appointment and resolve the issue without actually going to the office.

Field Audit - This is the audit most people dread. The IRS will ask you to provide documentation of various items on your return and meet with an IRS agent for a thorough review of your records. Be prepared to answer the auditor's questions, but don't volunteer information.

Taxpayer Compliance Measurement Program Audit - This rather lengthy and detailed audit asks you to document and prove every single item in your return. The IRS and Congress use the data from these audits for research and statistical purposes. These audits are arbitrary, and anyone can face them regardless of how carefully they prepare their tax returns.

Criminal-Investigation Audit - If you are suspected of tax evasion, the IRS will conduct a criminal-investigation audit. If they prove that you have purposefully not paid your income taxes, you can face substantial fines and even jail time. Obviously, you should retain qualified legal counsel if you encounter this type of audit.

The IRS - The IRS small business Website provides a wealth of information to small and growing businesses. A section for businesses getting off the ground includes a handy checklist and advice on choosing a business structure. It's particularly helpful on important topics such as employment taxes and business tax deductions. In addition, it has a list of small business resources with links to other government resources for small businesses. Obviously, you should retain qualified legal counsel if you face this type of audit. -*AllBusiness.com*

Important Small Business Tax Deduction Ideas:*

1. **Business Car Payment**

2. **Business Fuel**

3. **Business Meals & Entertainment**

4. **Business Travel**

5. **Business Education (Online classes, Books, Cd's, Success Seminars, Retreats, Conventions)**

6. **Business Auto Maintenance**

7. **Business Cell Phone**

8. **Business Cable, Internet**

9. **Business Awards**

10. **Miscellaneous Business Fees**

- *Actual Tax savings will, of course, be based on an individual basis. Please be sure to consult with a tax professional.

Deduct it Deduct it Deduct it!

Do you enjoy paying less in taxes? I know you do. Before you start swinging for the fences, get some of your money working for you in some sort of tax-deductible accounts like a 401K or SEP IRA account. Or better yet, why not put money into a Tax-FREE account like a ROTH IRA. I always say tax-deductible money and tax-deferred money are always better than taxable money.

Check this out... If you started a Roth IRA and invested $500 per month from age 25 to 67 @ 10% interest, you would accumulate 3.55 million! In a standard taxable account, you would only have $1.86 million! That's a tax savings of 1.69 million dollars! So, before you start investing, check out how you will be taxed on the money. Just one side note about taxes to keep in mind.

Always consider taxes but never make taxes your only reason for doing something. For example, I've heard people say, 'well, I don't want to make a bunch of money because then I'll have to pay a lot in taxes.' Well, that's pretty stupid, don't you think? I say, go make tons of money in the most tax-efficient places, stay financially organized so you can ultimately lower your bill to Uncle Sam or whoever your uncle is.

Keep it

You must know that it's not always about what you make; what you keep and invest in will determine your overall wealth and security. Use money to make more money. Like Shark Tank's Mr. Wonderful says, 'put those little money soldiers to work.' Protect them, so they can come back home safely!

A Note About Life Insurance

Buy the right kind of life insurance - Only buy TERM life insurance. Don't be fooled by those unscrupulous life insurance agents that love selling Whole life insurance. Consumer Reports, Money Magazine, LA Times, Personal Finance for Dummies, David Ramsey, Suze Orman, and countless books and articles recommend only buy term. Term life insurance is simple. You pay a premium; if you die within a particular period, the company pays the claim. No frills. No gimmicks. Always remember, if a salesperson offers you a life insurance product and you are confused, even slightly, do not buy. Life insurance is not rocket science. If you die, the company should pay the total amount of the policy.

Whole Life Insurance - Here's why Whole life insurance is a rip-off:

Life insurance and investments are bundled together. You should never commingle your investments and insurance into one package. Do you save with your auto insurance? No. Why not? So why would you save with your life insurance? Higher initial premium for same coverage. Term is always less costly. Purchasing the needed coverage for your family can be cost-prohibitive because the value is sometimes 10X more expensive. That means that if you die, you are giving your family much less money. Next, when you buy a whole life policy, you will, in most cases, generate a lower rate of return on investments due to fees, commissions, and expenses.

Why not just invest directly into the economy and bypass the middleman? That way, you get to keep more of your returns. Typically, a whole life policy will pay you 1-2% guaranteed. (forbes.com)

How about this fact... Typically, to access cash from the policy, you must borrow your money, which may cause the policy to lapse, at which time you would owe taxes on the gains that were part of the loan. Borrowing from your policy reduces the face amount available at death. First of all, if it's my money, why would I have to borrow my own money? Sounds "SUS" to me.

Did you know? Investing in a whole life policy is not the same as investing in a retirement plan such as an IRA or 401(k) account. The biggest difference is that you can deduct the money going into a 401K or SEP IRA. Tax-deductible money is always better than non-tax-deductible money, don't you think?

In summary: You get a lower return on savings, less protection for your family for more money, borrow money at a 6-8% interest, and potentially lose your savings if you die. Would you ever knowingly put your money into a policy like that? Lastly, consumer organizations do not recommend whole-life life insurance for families with few assets. If you haven't maxed out every tax-deductible investment program and diversified into other investments, don't even dare put your money into a policy like that.

The Theory of Decreasing Responsibility

According to the Theory of Decreasing Responsibility, your need for life insurance peaks along with your family responsibilities. When you're young, you may have children to support, a new mortgage payment, and many other obligations. Yet, you haven't had the time to accumulate much money. This is when the death of a breadwinner or caretaker could be devastating and when you need coverage the most. You usually have fewer dependents and fewer financial responsibilities when you're older. Plus, you've had years to accumulate wealth through savings and investments. At this point, your need for insurance has reduced dramatically, and you have your own funds to see you through your retirement years. This is why TERM is almost always the best insurance for most growing families.

Quick Question:

How would you feel if you created lasting and abundant wealth?

LAW 11 | CREATING LASTING WEALTH

"I actually think being an entrepreneur is a state of mind. If you're going to be an entrepreneur, my thesis is that you have to sacrifice everything for some period in your life to be successful. You have to be myopic and completely focused and unbalanced in every way. Once you've achieved success, you're free to do whatever you like."

Kevin O'Leary

Life should be abundant. It should be full of rich experiences. By rich, we don't mean just money; we mean living life and experiencing the nicer things in life to their full potential. When you generate massive lasting wealth, you can do this. You will be able to fly anywhere you want in the world, at any given moment. You will be able to help your family with whatever ideas, business ventures, and passions they wish to pursue. If your daughter or son wants to pursue sports, artistry, acting, singing, or creative arts, you will be able to back them - as well as allowing them to focus on mastering their skills without having to worry about making rent.

That is the true definition of wealth. This is what you should be striving for. Money is just a tool to elevate your life. It is the vehicle to bring you to your ultimate goal, which is to attain high vibrational energy full of unique experiences and memories. So, at the end of your journey, you will be able to die knowing you lived life to the max and set out to achieve everything you wanted to achieve. And ultimately passing on a legacy to your family.

REMEMBER WHY YOU STARTED; START WITH THE END IN MIND

To truly create massive lasting wealth, you need to understand one thing. Remember why you started and the higher purpose it will serve. Remember that the journey is not about chasing money; it's about attaining lasting freedom, security, experiencing life to its fullest capacity, and having the means to do so. Financial independence will allow you to be the person you truly want to be, without worrying about wearing a mask to fit in society or live in the matrix corporate world. It will provide you with the platform to pursue hobbies and things that truly set your soul on fire and fill you with joy.

Someone Will Need YOU One Day

For many years my mom has helped me with organizing my finances. Making sure the bills and taxes were paid on time. She used to tell me why do you save so much money? Why don't you spend more? I said, mom, 'one day somebody's going to need me. Somebody's going to need my help. It might be you or Dad or another family member. Or maybe just someone that is in dire straits. I don't know, but I save and invest and accumulate and create and build and grow and do more because one day somebody will need me.' As I'm writing this today, I just cut a check for $47,000. I won't discuss who or why I wrote the check for, but I did it because someone was in need. Someone was ill, and that $47,000 will save their life! If you can't write a check for $47,000 right now without blinking an eye, you need to get serious about building your wealth. And get ready because one day someone is gonna need you.

Well Frequency and Vibration for Life⚡⚡⚡

You always hear people saying, money can't buy happiness. I say, being broke doesn't buy you anything. There is no nobility in being poor, broke, and unable to provide for yourself or the people you love. Once you realign your mindset to align with the frequency of wealth, your entire existence and life experience will change.

In this life, we all live in different realities. Some experience a life of mediocrity because that is what they have been surrounded or born into. Some are born even worse off, in extreme poverty, or have lived in the direst circumstances. But remember, it is only one version of reality - in this world we live in. There is, and always will be, an abundance of wealth and riches in this world, waiting to be experienced. Whether in travel, food, homes, luxury lifestyle, clothes, cars, experiences, etc. The secret to being able to experience these more refined things in life is aligning to the 'wealth frequency of life.'

As said in previous chapters, to do this, you must harness the mindset and stay on the energy and frequency of wealth. You must be, speak, act and do as the wealthy do. You must adopt the same type of habits, daily routines, thought processes and surround yourself with people who are already wealthy, have built businesses, overcome trials, obstacles and have the wisdom and knowledge to help you also get there.

"Passive income is maintained with little to no work; it's not BUILT with little to no work."

Rachel Richards

Desperation

If you are not financially stable, you are desperate to make a buck. Always looking for your next sale. There's no safety net. People can tell when you're desperate; it's not where you want to be. Desperation is not sexy. Desperation does not attract; it repels. I've always said people can smell desperation a mile away. Be careful not to look desperate. It's not a good look. The more financially successful you become, the easier it is to win business. This is because your confidence shines when you don't need a sale. That confidence is why people will want to do business with you. This is one of the biggest reasons why when you really get your money right, bigger piles of money come looking for you!

Alignment

On an energetic level, people should understand that vibrations are carried out and felt through the subconscious level. If you think about frequencies, they carry like radio waves on a radio channel. If you are not tapped into that channel, there is no possibility that you can connect or align with others, situations, or opportunities on that same channel. If you are not in the mindset of abundance and wealth, you cannot possibly attract it. This is also why it's so important to spend time with successful people so that you can fall in alignment. That alignment is why the rich keep getting richer.

Energy is contagious, and so is the mindset of wealth and abundance. The more you are around an environment that concerns wealth-building and prosperity, you will be habituated into thinking it's normal. You have to find your people that will facilitate this growth and are already where you want to be. Your job after that is just to connect, align and watch your life unfold and change forever. You will start speaking the language and thinking the same and developing the 'wealth' mindset and vibration. From that, relationships will be forged, and your greatness will emerge.

Multiply Your Way to Freedom

Create multiple income streams.

If you haven't already figured out, this book stresses creating multiple income streams by replicating and duplicating. Other multiple income streams include rental property, stock investments, options trading, Amazon drop shipping efforts, cryptocurrency trading, etc.

You see, the power of multiple streams of income is immense. Warren Buffett said we should always create multiple income streams to make money while sleeping. The average millionaire has seven streams of income. Think about it, your job is just one stream of income. But what if you get sick? Laid off? Fired? These are all situations you can't control.

There's no security in a job. Doesn't that worry you? It should. If you need a job right now, that's wonderful, but investigating ways to broaden your income streams is one of the most important things you can do today. Find out what you love and focus on making that an income stream. With that said, let's dive into some ways you can start building some massive passive income . . .

Stock Market ⊿

I love the stock market. I've been invested in the stock market for twenty-five years now and love the prospect of buying and trading stocks. I can trade on up markets and down markets even when the market is trading sideways, I can make money. Ever since I started trading covered calls on my existing stocks, I've added tens of thousands of dollars per month!

I'm not here to tell you how to invest as this is not an investment advice book, but if you have large quantities of shares in companies that are companies that you probably won't sell anytime soon, don't you think that you should be generating a stream of income from those stocks? You say, 'but I'm already pulling in dividends from the stocks.' That's great, but did you know you can run a covered call on your existing shares and pull in actual gains?

That strategy is probably one of the most overlooked strategies by people that currently own large quantities of stocks. I challenge you to learn more. You will be surprised by how safe that strategy is. So, you say you want to play it really safe?

Your best option is a good ol' Mutual Fund. Whether it's aggressive, balanced, or conservative, there is a fund with your name on it. You see, a mutual fund is just a collection of stocks, bonds, and cash that is professionally managed by some brilliant dudes and dudettes! They take millions and billions of shareholders' money and spread it across hundreds of different companies, such as Apple, Microsoft, Disney, Home Depot, Amazon, Tesla, etc.

In most cases, no more than 5% of the money would go into a single stock. That way, if the stock goes to zero, you wouldn't lose all your money. Plus, you have the opportunity to make way better gains than the bank. I have recommended mutual funds that have paid, on average, per year, 10% since 1960. Pretty cool, huh?

Property & Rentals 🏠

Speaking of places to help you legally lower your tax bill. Let's talk about property. Land and property are ways to build extreme long-term wealth and, of course, passive income. Back in 2006, my lease ran out for my financial services location. I was very tempted to just lease out another place, but I decided to purchase after a bad negotiation with the landlord. That decision has made me more than $1 million in total profit, all the while watching the property value of the building plummet and then skyrocket before my eyes. The truth is I bought the building at completely the wrong time.

A couple of years after my purchase, the whole world collapsed in 2008! One of the worst property value declines in the history of the world. I purchased my building for $1.1 million, and at one point, it was worth $600,000. But one thing I realized is that no matter what, people needed office space. So, through the years, I was still collecting rents on the building.

Over the last fifteen years, those rents have paid me over $1 million. Not to mention the property value as of this writing is worth 1.6 million. So, if you add $500,000 in property value growth and another million in rental income, that comes out to $1.5

million. And I expect the building to increase in value over time simply because it's in a prime location. I expect rental income to be consistent because companies always need extra office space.

So don't panic if the market declines dramatically. Your goal is to create cash flow. Today the building is completely paid off. Today most of every dime collected is profit. A mentor of mine, Grant Cardone, always said, 'nobody's manufacturing new dirt.' Real estate, multi-family units, apartment buildings will always be incredible opportunities to generate real and lasting cash flow that never stops!

Building an Investment Portfolio

Although this is not a how-to investment book, I want to make sure that you continually stay organized in building your portfolio. Although I don't believe in dramatic diversification, I believe that multiple sources of investments can help shield in different times of the market. For example, I own real estate, and I own stocks. As long as the real estate brings in cash flow, it really doesn't matter what happens to the overall market. I can trade stocks in up-and-down markets, so the overall market does not deter me from trading and generating profit again.

Some might say, 'well, wonder if your stocks are going down?' That's OK; I'm a long-term investor. I understand cycles, and I know the market will go up and down. Some markets are worse than others. Some cycles are more devastating than others. That's OK. As long as I'm generating cash flow, that's what matters. Thirty years from now, my objectives might be different. I might say one day, well, it's time to sell everything and put it all into safe annuities at 5%. Who knows? The point is that wherever you're at in your life, you need an actual plan and portfolio of investments that make you money, whether you're working or not.

Always Look for Opportunities

Take calculated risks. I believe there is no wealth without risk. The more risk you take, the more potential for wealth. Most of you would agree with that, right? I just want to encourage you to always take calculated risks. What's a calculated risk? It's a potential investment risk that you understand. Years ago, I learned about stocks, and a very famous Fidelity portfolio manager said to invest in what you know.

If you do not understand technology or cryptocurrency, or the Meta-Verse, you have no business investing in those areas. I feel comfortable investing in technology companies, computer companies, and graphic card companies because I understand the space. I invest in the number one electric car company simply because I have three of their cars. I understand it for me, it's a volatile stock, and there is much risk involved. Still, I believe in the long-term strategy and philosophy of the company. So, therefore, I feel comfortable going to bed at night knowing that even if the stock takes a deep dive, I will be OK in the long run. I'm hedging my investment if I can pull in hundreds of thousands of dollars in premium over the long term from covered call options, although the stock might be going down. So, when you make investments, learn all you can about those investments.

Learn about the companies and do research. Understand what you're investing in. Years ago, I took $100,000 and dumped it into a highly speculative investment with some people who had a great idea, but I knew very little about the company. I knew little about where the company was based. I knew little about the management team, and I knew little about the downfalls of investing in a starter company. Those hundred thousand dollars is now in the graveyard. Some people might say, well, you lost $100,000! I say that was $100,000 tuition in startup investing. And so next time someone comes to you and says, hey, I want you to invest in my startup company, you say, give me all the details. Research your butt off. Get to know anything and everything about that company before you even think about writing a check.

By the way, if you've never heard of asymmetrical investing, it's an idea that many wealthy people believe in. It says that you make lots of very risky bets knowing that some of them you will lose everything, some of them you won't make very much, but there might be one or two that makes so much money that all of the gains will overcome any losses of the past.

Cryptocurrency 💰

I just wanted to take a brief moment to explain why I believe in cryptocurrency. What is cryptocurrency? Cryptocurrency is best considered digital currency (it only exists on computers). It is transferred between peers (there is no middleman like a bank). Transactions are recorded on a digital public ledger (called a "blockchain"). Transaction data and the ledger are encrypted using cryptography (which is why it is called "crypto" "currency"). It is decentralized, meaning it is controlled by users and computer algorithms and not a central government. It is distributed, meaning the blockchain is hosted on many computers across the globe.

Meanwhile, cryptocurrencies are traded on online cryptocurrency exchanges, like stock exchanges. Bitcoin (commonly traded under the symbol BTC) is one of many cryptocurrencies. Other cryptocurrencies have names like "Ether (ETH)," "Ripple (XRP)," and "Litecoin (LTC)." Alternatives to Bitcoin are called "altcoins." Here's a quick summary . . .

- Cryptocurrency can be a digital currency like PayPal or bank credit (what you use with your credit or debit card).

- Cryptocurrency transactions and balances are recorded on a public digital ledger called a blockchain.

- Cryptocurrencies can be accessed through software called wallets (transactions are broadcast to the network to be added to the blockchain via transactions created in wallets). This can be equated to online banking (where you have account numbers and passwords and move funds between accounts).

- Cryptocurrencies can be bought through a broker or traded on online cryptocurrency exchanges (like a stock exchange).

- There are many other cryptocurrencies beyond Bitcoin (some of which are better defined as digital assets).

- Unlike bank credit, which represents a centrally controlled and issued fiat currency (like the US dollar), cryptocurrency is decentralized and thus not centrally controlled.

- Instead of a central power controlling cryptocurrency, an algorithm and users themselves control cryptocurrency.

- The algorithm dictates how transactions work and how new coins are created. Users create peer-to-peer transactions using software called wallets. Transactions are recorded on a public digital ledger.

- Those who confirm transactions by breaking cryptographic codes are called miners. Mining is a process that creates new coins.

Of course, you don't need to know any of that. If you chose, all you need to do is set up an account and buy and sell Bitcoin, Bitcoin Cash, Ether, or Litecoin and send and receive cryptocurrency. You can get more information at *Cryptocurrencyfacts.com.*

Believe it or not, a friend of mine told me about Cryptocurrency years ago. I told him that I didn't believe in Crypto. It was probably a scam. What a mistake! If I had invested $100K, that 100K would now be worth $20 million today! Although I don't sell cryptocurrency and I am surely *not* trying to get you to invest in cryptocurrency, I do want you to be fully aware that, in my opinion, the Blockchain, Bitcoin and other cryptocurrencies are viable technologies that are the future!

"If you don't believe it or don't get it, I don't have the time to try to convince you, sorry."

Satoshi Nakamoto, Creator of Bitcoin

THE GOAL OF GENERATIONAL WEALTH

As you know, wealth rarely lasts much further than grandchildren. Taxes, expenses, dilution of the well-being of children and their children, and the inevitable corruption of large amounts of money ultimately affect family conditions.

Yet the Rockefeller family challenged all of this. According to Forbes, the Rockefeller family, now in its seventh generation, have maintained a significant fortune – in 2016, their wealth stash was $ 11 billion. This happened more than 100 years after John D. Rockefeller became America's first billionaire after founding the Standard Oil Company in the late 19th century. Even more unlikely, the family remained largely cohesive, without public scandals, hostility, lawsuits, and tragedies typical to other golden dynasties. Currently, over 250 family members are direct descendants of John D. Rockefeller and Laura Spelman Rockefeller.

Why Build Lasting Wealth?

Lasting wealth is the security you will provide for yourself and your family. I remember a thirty-something prospect telling me, 'Well, I don't really need to save for the future because I've decided I will work until I die.' I said that's great, but what if your BODY decides otherwise?

The point is that none of us can 100% tell the future. Could we get an illness? What about a car accident that leaves us alive but unable to work? What if a family member needs money for a major medical procedure? Becoming financially stable is a decision that you must make today. Keeping, preserving, growing that money that will last generations will be a decision you will make on a continual basis.

Cut down expenses, refinance your debt, get additional sources of income – do what needs to be done to make any monthly contributions to your investment accounts as non-negotiable as your car payment.

Treat Your LIFE, Like A real Business.

Every business tracks its spending. Why not you?

Every business attempts to lower taxes. Why not you?

Every business focuses on growing revenue. Why not you?

Every business builds its assets. Why not you?

Run Your Finances Like a Corporation

People ask me where did you put your money, where did you invest it? My main focus early on was to build up my savings.

#1 is to have a solid emergency fund. Then move that money into tax-deductible programs, SEP IRAs, 401Ks, aggressive mutual funds, real estate, and individual stocks, of course, and make sure that I also invested back into my business. I was never cheap when investing in my business. BTW… my corporation is the most lucrative investment I've ever made. As of this writing, it's worth about $10M and pays me $1 million-plus per year passively.

After all is said and done, I've been able to pay off my 5000 square-foot building. I have paid off rental property, a beautiful, almost paid-off multi-million-dollar home (my mortgage is $1,800 per month). And, I have millions in a stock portfolio that pay me big money every month passively through dividends, capital gains, appreciation, and options. I've been able to amass a net worth of

$20 million! And the best part? I feel like I'm just beginning my real money-making years.

It's funny because I was just telling a friend that I've never felt so positive, so in alignment with the Universe. So sure of the future. The best is yet to come!

Can you now see why creating massive lasting wealth is crucial to living a full life? Can you now see how the matrix and corporate world have sought to keep people slaving for the system and keep you contained in mediocrity and mediocre experiences? You have nothing to lose and everything to win when you are open to pursuing wealth and purpose. You will gain freedom, you will gain happiness, you will gain joy. You will be able to create a lasting legacy by elevating those around you and providing them with rich experiences and prosperous life. Because life is meant to be abundant! Life is meant to be lived. Life is intended for progress.

Now go get that pot of GOLD!

Action Steps I Will Take Today to Change My Life!

1._____

_____

2._____

_____

3._____

_____

4._____

_____

5._____

_____

6._____

_____

7._____

_____

8._____

_____

9._____

_____

10_____

_____

11._____

WEALTH ON THE BEACH
THE ONLINE COURSE!
11 UNIVERSAL LAWS TO BUILDING FINANCIAL FREEDOM
-GAIN DEEPER INSIGHT TO THE 11 UNIVERSAL LAWS
ON VIDEO AND ON DEMAND!
-HOW DANIEL THINKS AND APPLYS THE LAWS
-SPECIFICALLY, HOW HE WON FINANCIALLY.
-DIVE INTO THE WORLD OF QUANTUM PHYSICS, MONEY,
INVESTING AND BUSINESS THROUGH DANIEL'S EYES.
-GO TO WEALTHONTHEBEACH.COM FOR ALL THE DETAILS

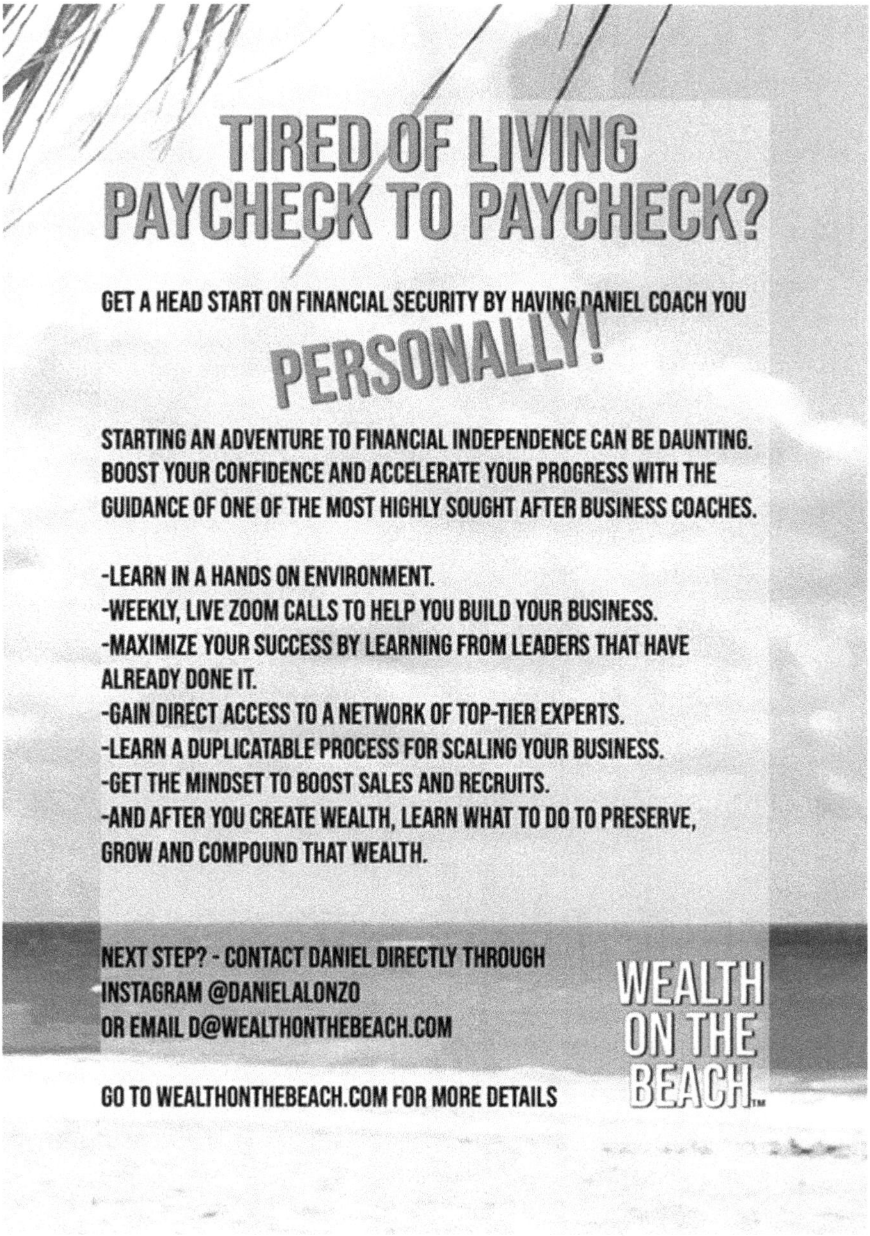
TIRED OF LIVING
PAYCHECK TO PAYCHECK?
GET A HEAD START ON FINANCIAL SECURITY BY HAVING DANIEL COACH YOU
PERSONALLY!
STARTING AN ADVENTURE TO FINANCIAL INDEPENDENCE CAN BE DAUNTING. BOOST YOUR CONFIDENCE AND ACCELERATE YOUR PROGRESS WITH THE GUIDANCE OF ONE OF THE MOST HIGHLY SOUGHT AFTER BUSINESS COACHES.
-LEARN IN A HANDS ON ENVIRONMENT.
-WEEKLY, LIVE ZOOM CALLS TO HELP YOU BUILD YOUR BUSINESS.
-MAXIMIZE YOUR SUCCESS BY LEARNING FROM LEADERS THAT HAVE ALREADY DONE IT.
-GAIN DIRECT ACCESS TO A NETWORK OF TOP-TIER EXPERTS.
-LEARN A DUPLICATABLE PROCESS FOR SCALING YOUR BUSINESS.
-GET THE MINDSET TO BOOST SALES AND RECRUITS.
-AND AFTER YOU CREATE WEALTH, LEARN WHAT TO DO TO PRESERVE, GROW AND COMPOUND THAT WEALTH.
NEXT STEP? - CONTACT DANIEL DIRECTLY THROUGH
INSTAGRAM @DANIELALONZO
OR EMAIL D@WEALTHONTHEBEACH.COM
GO TO WEALTHONTHEBEACH.COM FOR MORE DETAILS
WEALTH ON THE BEACH TM

ACKNOWLEDGEMENTS

This book is 25 years in the making. Lots of adventures and lessons. Tons of advice taken. Many sleepless nights included.

How does a person say "thank you" when there are so many people to thank?

First & foremost, Karma. A true partner and love from the beginning.

To my mom, who taught me kindness, love and positivity.

My Dad & my Pop. Thank you both.

Max and Ava. I love you and I'm so proud of you.

Kasey Phoenix Casal. Grateful for all your help.

Jesus. I pray you continue to guide my life.

To all my mentors and friends… You know who you are.

And my editor, Andrea Lard at The Creative 5280, who settled the question of 'to' or 'for.'

Lastly, I'm very grateful for YOU the reader. Serving people has always been my passion. It's my life's work. Thank you for supporting me and helping to make my dream come true.

LEGAL DISCLAIMER

Wealth on the Beach Book, Daniel Alonzo & Kasey Phoenix Casal (Authors) assert that this book & links associated are for informational purposes only. Use of and access to the book, Site and the information, materials, services, books, courses and other content available on or through the book, Site ("Content") are subject to these terms of use and all applicable laws.

NO INVESTMENT ADVICE

The Content of this book is for informational purposes only, you should not construe any such information or other material as legal, tax, investment, financial, or other advice. Nothing contained constitutes a solicitation, recommendation, endorsement, or offer by named above or any third party service provider to buy or sell any securities or other financial instruments in this or in in any other jurisdiction in which such solicitation or offer would be unlawful under the securities laws of such jurisdiction.

All Content in this book is information of a general nature and does not address the circumstances of any particular individual or entity. Nothing in the book constitutes professional and/or financial advice, nor does any information constitute a comprehensive or complete statement of the matters discussed or the law relating thereto. Authors are not fiduciaries by virtue of any person's use. You alone assume the sole responsibility of evaluating the merits and risks associated with the use of any information or other content that the authors provide before making any decisions based on such information or other Content. In exchange for you having access to this book, you agree not to hold the authors, its affiliates or any third party service provider liable for any possible claim for damages arising from any decision you make based on information or other Content made available to you through this book.

INVESTMENT RISKS

There are risks associated with investing in securities. Investing in stocks, bonds, options, real estate, exchange traded funds, mutual funds, and money market funds involve risk of loss. Loss of principal is possible. Some high risk investments may use leverage, which will accentuate gains & losses. Foreign investing involves special risks, including a greater volatility and political, economic and currency risks and differences in accounting methods. A security's or a firm's past investment performance is not a guarantee or predictor of future investment performance.

THANK YOU FOR BUYING THIS BOOK!

I appreciate all of your feedback and love hearing what you have to say.

Please leave me a helpful review on Amazon letting me know what you thought of the book. I appreciate you!

LET'S CONNECT.

Please feel free to DM me directly through my Instagram page.

I am built to serve YOU.

Subscribe and Follow on Social Media!

Wealthonthebeach.com

Alonzoacademy.com

Youtube - Daniel Alonzo

iTunes & Spotify - Wealth on the Beach Podcast

Instagram - @danielalonzo

Facebook - Daniel Alonzo

TikTok - DanielAlonzo100

Linkedin - Daniel Alonzo

Twitter - DanielAlonzoBL

Truth Social - @danielalonzo

www.ingramcontent.com/pod-product-compliance
Lightning Source LLC
Chambersburg PA
CBHW070041100426
42740CB00013B/2749